A STEAMBOAT NAMED
SABINO

A STEAMBOAT NAMED

SABINO

GEORGE KING III

MYSTIC SEAPORT

MYSTIC, CONNECTICUT

1999

MYSTIC SEAPORT, MYSTIC, CT 06355-0990

Printed in the United States of America

Cataloging in Publication data:

King, George, 1947–
    A Steamboat Named Sabino / by George King III–1st ed.–Mystic, Conn. :
Mystic Seaport, 1999.
    p. : ill., plans, ports. ; cm.
    Includes bibliographical references and index.

1. Sabino (Steamboat) 2. Steamboats. I Title.

VM383.S2K56

ISBN 0-913372-87-0

Designed and produced by Ben Kann, New Haven, Connecticut
Illustrations credited to M.S.M. are in the collections of Mystic Seaport

CONTENTS

DEDICATED TO THOSE WHO PRESERVE MARITIME SKILLS

ACKNOWLEDGEMENTS

RESEARCH FOR THIS BOOK snuck up on me. I first had to learn enough about *Sabino*'s history to answer visitors' questions as they rode the old steamer at Mystic Seaport. As I delved into the records and correspondence in the registrar's office, questions were answered but more questions were posed. Contradictory information and sea-stories of questionable accuracy motivated me to find the "real story" behind the variations. In pursuing the answers, I found myself immersed in a research project of unanticipated depth.

My search took me through much of New England as the *Sabino* story unfolded. The many generous people I encountered along the way made this an enjoyable, albeit rather long, voyage. I want here to recognize some of the many contributors to the story of *A Steamboat Named Sabino*.

Paul & Mimi Aldrich, Bristol, Maine

Dave & Betsey Andrews, South Bristol, Maine

Jim & Irene Corbin, Salisbury, Massachusetts

Nicholas Dean, Edgecomb, Maine

Captain Jamieson Findlay, Portland, Maine

William A. Kelsey, South Bristol, Maine

Jim Millinger, Woods Hole, Massachusetts

Barbara Rumsey, Boothbay Region Historical Society, Boothbay Harbor, Maine

Skidompha Library, Damariscotta, Maine

Steamship Historical Society of America, Providence, Rhode Island

Jane W. Stevens, Popham Beach, Maine

Contributors who provided photographs are acknowledged following the caption of each image. Letters and additional reference materials can be found in the *Sabino* files at Mystic Seaport's registrar's office.

I would also like to thank some special people who took their time to help in the preparation of this manuscript.

Lisa Horan, Groton, Connecticut

Rich Voss, Staten Island, New York

And most of all I would like to thank my family, Kathy, George IV, Elizabeth, and David, for their continued patience and support through the entire project.

Oyster shell mounds on the banks of the Damariscotta River testify to the bountiful harvest enjoyed by Native Americans prior to the arrival of European settlers in the State of Maine. (Postcard from the author's collection)

CHAPTER 1

BEFORE THE LAUNCHING

N TELLING THE STORY of *Sabino*, we will begin with time and place before her launching. From this perspective, we will have an appreciation of daily life in coastal Maine. By understanding the transportation challenges facing the inhabitants of this region, we will see why there were more than 1,000 small passenger steamers* registered in the year of *Sabino*'s launching.[1] In order to get a running start at the *Sabino* story, let us back up to the last quarter of the nineteenth century.

For generations, only the rich could afford a summer retreat. New money and old money could be found summering and rusticating in the 1880s and 1890s from the Adirondacks to Newport, and the "cottages" and "camps" of the rich and famous survive today as testimony to the extravagance of the era. Vacationers to the coast of Maine during the nineteenth century came from the moneyed end of urban society. By 1890 Bar Harbor had "turned

into a summer colony of New York."[2] The popular society pages of local newspapers documented the doings of such Down East visitors; meanwhile, there were unheralded vacationers enjoying the same scenery if not the same privileges.

The innovations of the industrial age brought changes to Victorian society on a variety of fronts, and several social developments emerged that had not existed before. Although the industrialization of America has often been blamed for grave social injustices, it was also the catalyst for some social advancements. Significant among these was the institution of regular work hours and scheduled days off. This structured work environment, coupled with a 40-percent increase in purchasing power between 1850 and 1880,[3] resulted in a new phenomenon we have come to call leisure activity.

For the first time in our history, the working man could count on a little time away from his job. Those with only Sundays or weekends off could enjoy the pleasures of the beach and the amusement park. These fantasy lands of rides and games were often constructed by railroads or streetcar companies at the ends of their

*By actual count there were 1,010 small passenger steamers listed in the 1908 *Merchant Vessel List*. A small passenger steamer is one of less than 100 tons, excluding ferryboats.

The Menawarmet Hotel at Boothbay Harbor was one of numerous hotels and boarding houses that provided lodging, meals and recreational activity for Victorian-era vacationers to Maine. (Postcard from the author's collection)

lines, a gambit that attracted ridership on days when workers were not traveling to and from their places of employment. Ocean Beach in Connecticut and Norumbega Park and Lincoln Park in Massachusetts are examples of this development.

Mills, factories, and other industrial work places often closed for a week or two each year to service machinery that was inaccessible during normal operations. Employees would find themselves with no work during these periods, but for working-class and middle-class breadwinners this week or so away from the routine was new and welcome leisure time. Through judicious planning, above-average scrimping, and re-directing a dollar or two from the egg money, many an American family found that they could enjoy a seven-day summer vacation on the rock-bound coast of Maine.

Another variety of tourist was the sportsman. These seasonal outdoorsmen liked to venture inland to the lakes and streams of Maine's interior, hunting in the pine woods, fishing the lakes and streams. They often traveled by canoe with a "Maine guide." Both tourist and guide would board a night or more at the home of a farmer who was willing to provide a simple room for a simple price. Soon enough the year-round residents saw the financial wisdom in letting rooms. Entrepreneurial natives built additions to their farmhouses to accommodate the increasing number of seasonal visitors.

As the lure of northern New England increased, the demand for rooms soon outgrew the space available in the farmer's ell. By 1875, hotels began to be built in the mountains and on the shore. At first, the resort hotel was a simple affair with a parlor as the gathering place, much like today's small "bed and breakfast" inns. There were no organized activities to occupy the guests, and vacationers were free to find their own entertainment.[4] Senior guests would often perch in the rocking chairs provided by the hotel and keep an eye on the younger members of the family as they explored the acres surrounding the inn. These venerable members of the "rocking-chair fleet" were quick to keep the youngsters in line–either members their own clan or children from another visiting family.

As competition among the hotels increased, publishers issued guides which reported on the accommodations of each hotel, and hotels became bigger and busier. New England entrepreneurs built hotels at the most pic-turesque locations that money could buy, and the newer and bigger places were truly resorts. These early mountain and seaside resorts attracted those who wanted to enjoy the seashore or the North Woods while still experiencing the comforts of home. To get to these out-of–the-way vacation spots, travelers would arrive by train at the nearest depot and then make their way by whatever means available to their chosen hotel or resort. Hotel owners recognized that the success of their resorts depended largely on access to the railroad, and they were quick to devise secondary modes of transportation to connect with the trains for the convenience of their guests. Horse-drawn conveyances were the most common. Hotels such as the old Chadbourne House on Sebago Lake were serviced by four-horse Concord coaches which "jolted the summer visitor to his destination."[5] Horse-drawn coaches continued to convey summer guests to resort communities into the 1920s.

The more enterprising landlords employed innovations of the time's advancing technology. Appolos Smith built an electric railway to transport guests from the Delaware and Hudson Railroad's depot at Lake Clear Junction to his Adirondack resort hotel at Paul Smiths.* This unique electric car could deliver visitors with all their baggage or simply couple onto their private railroad car and bring them to the resort without the passengers even changing seats. Not only did Smith own the hotel and the railway but he also owned the hydroelectric station that provided the power for both.

One of the most peculiar and long-lived resort conveyances in New England is the Mount Washington cog

---

*When I attended Paul Smith's College in the 1960s this electric car was still to be seen on the college property. It is noteworthy that its predecessor, a stagecoach, still exists. In recent years, volunteers have restored the coach to operating condition.

railway. The "cog" is so named because of its tractive mechanism. The mountain is so steep that conventional wheels would slip on the grade. Inventor Sylvester Marsh installed a gear or cog on the axle between the driving wheels of the locomotive. This cog meshes with a toothed track between the conventional rails and provides the necessary traction to carry the train upward. For 13 decades this unique steam-powered contraption has clawed its way to the peak of New England's most prominent mountain, where the Summit House has welcomed visitors since 1869. It is still in operation today.

The coast of Maine is a labyrinth of terrestrial talons reaching seaward into the North Atlantic, a fringe of peninsulas accompanied by countless islands. Some islands are no more than rocks, while others are large enough to host independent communities. The view from any one of these sea-washed peninsulas or islands as the fingers of dawn reach through the darkness bringing light and life to the coast of Maine is an inspirational experience. It is on these rugged peninsulas and islands that entrepreneurial Mainers built their hotels.

The distance between neighboring capes on the Maine coast is often less than a mile; however, to travel by land from one to another can often require a trip of 20 miles or more. Locals would simply jump into a boat and row or sail across: for the curious visitor bent on exploring an adjacent point of land, the tart reply of "Ya can't get theyah from heeyah" was often more fact than Down East humor.

Up and down the coast of Maine in the last decades of the nineteenth century the need arose for a waterborne conveyance that was small enough to get over the bottom at low tide and nimble enough to weave its way into the tightest of landings. It had to be large enough to carry passengers, bags and baggage, and light freight to supply the islands. It needed to be powerful enough to overcome the variable winds and the relentless currents, yet simple enough for a small crew to operate safely and within a reasonable budget. The evolutionary result was the small passenger steamboat or ferry.

But just what is a steamboat? Essentially, a vessel simply needs to be propelled in whole or in part by steam to be a steamboat. However, the term is annoyingly vague considering the variety of sizes and functions of steam-powered vessels. It is similar in its broad scope to categorizing a vehicle simply as a "truck." To some, a truck is a sporty pick-up that will never see a load in its pristine bed, while to others it is a tandem tractor-trailer rig carrying tons of freight across the country. The variety in types of steamboats is similar. To define the steamboat it may help to determine what a steamboat is not. It is not a steamship. Steamships are vessels that travel across oceans and are capable of carrying passengers and cargo between countries. These goliaths of the sea were either propelled by large paddle wheels mounted on each side of the ship or by conventional screw propellers in the nineteenth century. In either case, the appearance of "S.S."–for steam ship–before the name of the vessel is appropriate.

Another class of steam-powered vessels active during the nineteenth century and into the twentieth was the "sound steamer." These popular vessels carried passengers and cargo between New York City and various ports on Long Island Sound. Although these vessels reached lengths in excess of 400 feet, carried more than 2,000 passengers, and could be pushed by engines that developed more than 11,000 horsepower, they were still considered steamboats, and were always referred to as such by their officers and crews.[6] These vessels could likewise be sidewheel- or screw-propelled.

The designation of "S.S." was conspicuously absent from the names of sound steamers and lesser vessels.

The prefix "Steamer" or the abbreviation "Str." is most often found in references or descriptions on postcards of steamboats from this period. In fact, vessel enrollments from the period list these smaller craft as "steamers," illustrating government sanction for the term. The term "steamboat" covers a variety of craft that includes Mississippi (more correctly Western River) sidewheelers and sternwheelers, recreational steam launches, small passenger steamers and steam-powered ferryboats, among others.

Ferry is another semi-ambiguous nautical term. To most, a ferry is a double-ended boat most often powered by machinery. It is usually capable of carrying vehicles that drive in one end and out the other. But a second type of vessel also bears the ferry name. It is a small powered vessel used to ferry passengers to and from island or coastal points, usually to a larger terminal on the mainland. These passenger ferries were common to the islands and inlets of northern New England.

Small passenger ferries made their appearance in Maine waters during the 1880s. By the turn of the century they were flitting here and there along the coast like mosquitoes in a rain barrel. They would meet the train and transport passengers to the hotels along the rivers and inlets of their own section of coastline. They would bring freight and supplies of food and ice to the resorts and to private landings along the way. Many held mail contracts and displayed the distinctive blue and white "U.S. Mail" flag from their jackstaffs. It was not uncommon for such a little vessel to make ten round trips per day while meeting its varied responsibilities during the busy summer months.[7] With the advent of mail contracts, the steamboats were required to run as long into the fall and winter as possible. Likewise, they had to start operations as soon as the ice was out of their rivers. When the rivers were frozen, a wagon or sleigh delivered mail.

With the extended operating season required by the mail came a new benefit for downriver residents: The steamboat could now provide transportation for high school students who were required to travel "in town" for their secondary education. There were other benefits. These boats were the trucks and buses of their day. The small steamer was the mass-transit vehicle on coasts and rivers at the turn of the century. Passengers could flag down the passing boat from any landing, or they could arrange to have goods picked up "in town" and delivered on the next regular run, to island outposts, river and peninsular villages, even to coastal and riverside farms.

It would be many years before paved roads and privately owned vehicles would change this picturesque transportation system. This was the era of the small steamboat in all its grand simplicity.

Anodyne was the water-borne equivalent of a peddler's cart. Mr. Johnson used the 36-foot steamer to promote his Anodyne Liniment at the many landings along the Damariscotta River between 1895 and 1899. (Boothbay Region Historical Society)

CHAPTER 2

TO MARKET A PRODUCT

A CLASSIC EXAMPLE OF A transportation system developed by a fleet of small steamboats can be found on the Damariscotta River in Maine. Flowing southward 14 miles from a lake bearing the same name, the Damariscotta empties into the Atlantic some 50 miles north of Portland. Like most coastal estuaries, it is dotted with picturesque villages whose names evoke calendar images of New England. Boothbay Harbor, Christmas Cove, Pemaquid Beach, as well as Damariscotta itself, are recognized far from the Pine Tree State as typical Maine coastal communities.

The region was an important area for fishing and shellfish gathering long before the English arrived. A shell mound on the shore of the Damariscotta River remains as silent testimony to the bountiful harvest of clams and oysters that attracted Native Americans to its banks. When European settlers arrived, they were attracted by the same resources. Fishermen worked from seasonal camps on the islands and peninsulas of the Maine coast and their catch provided food for local consumption as well as for export to the Boston market.

In the 1800s visitors arrived to enjoy recreational fishing and hunting, and the summer abundance and beauty of the area captivated them. The era of Maine as "Vacationland" had begun.

As we drive through Maine on today's highways, we are bombarded with advertisements. These marketing tools come in the form of radio commercials, billboards, and even painted signs on the sides of trucks to promote the truck owner's product or service. Long before the days of radio, trucks, and billboards, the Yankee entrepreneur was no less creative. One such master of advertising was the maker of Johnson's Anodyne Liniment.

The name of the product had been carefully chosen to induce a sense of well-being. Anodyne, as an adjective, means soothing or relaxing. The nominative form comes from the Latin "anodynus" meaning "without pain." A more appropriate name for a liniment could hardly be found.

Johnson's Anodyne Liniment was promoted as the "remedy for every ailment from colds to dandruff."[1] A 1908 ad enumerated the benefits of the elixir as a cure for "...colds, croup, coughs, catarrh, cramps, cholera,

Anodyne was the first boat of the Damariscotta Steamboat Company's fleet. In preparation for passenger service her machinery was moved forward and her pilothouse was raised. At some point after 1907, the cabin was removed leaving just a canopy with open decks to catch the cool summer breeze. (Boothbay Region Historical Society)

colic, asthma, bronchitis, influenza, and pleurisy."[2] The ad announced that Johnson's miraculous product "...for 97 years has cured sprains, strains, muscular rheumatism, sciatica, lumbago, stiff joints, lame back, etc."[3]

As early as 1811 the liniment was sold all along the Maine coast. To aid in marketing and distributing his product, Mr. Johnson had a boat built that was similar in function to today's delivery van. It provided transportation for cargos of liniment and also served as a mobile billboard.

Johnson's steamer was launched from the A & M Gamage yard in Bristol in 1895. The boat was a modest 36' long, 9.97' breadth, and 4.3' draft, with a gross tonnage of 13. Her official number was 107163.[4] Appropriately named *Anodyne*, she was powered by a single-cylinder engine[5] that received steam from a boiler that was already three years old when installed in the boat.[6] The name of the vessel, and likewise the product, was displayed from name-boards on each side of the bow, on both sidelight boxes, and on the transom. There were signs on each side of the superstructure just aft of the wheelhouse that read, "Johnson's Anodyne Liniment, Every Mother Should Have It In The House." An additional sign proclaiming the virtue of the product was mounted atop the pilothouse to ensure that oncoming vessels would not miss the message.[7]

Captain Elliot P. Gamage was master of the new vessel, and George Farrow of Tenants Harbor was the engineer. A young deckhand by the name of Ernest Hart completed *Anodyne*'s crew.[8] On her maiden voyage upriver to Damariscotta, Mr. Johnson joined *Anodyne*'s regular crew.*

She was a busy little boat for a few years, homeported at South Bristol. Captain Gamage had an arrangement with the owners that allowed him to use the boat for private parties when not engaged in the business of peddling liniment.[9]

By 1900, Johnson's Anodyne Liniment was well-established in coastal Maine. It could be found in most any general store, and wide acceptance of the product brought a diminished need for *Anodyne* as an advertising tool.[10] Captain Gamage saw his employment as a liniment drummer coming to a close. Encouraged by the success of the charters on *Anodyne*, Gamage purchased the boat and modified it to better suit the tourist trade.

On June 1, 1900, *Anodyne* entered into daily service between Damariscotta and Christmas Cove, touching on the intermediate landings of East Boothbay, South Bristol and Heron Island.[11] In addition to scheduled service, Captain Gamage actively sought charter work. One of the first excursions under his ownership was a picnic trip for the Boy's Choir of Saint Andrew's Episcopal Church of Newcastle.†

---

*A photograph from the collection of James Stevens, published in *Kennebec, Boothbay Harbor Steamboat Album*, shows Mr. Johnson standing amidships on *Anodyne*. Captain and Mrs. Gamage are on the foredeck. The other two people in the photo are not identified, but I suspect that the young man at the stern is Ernest Hart. The tall man just forward of Hart may be George Farrow, but I do not know if any self-respecting engineer would be that far from the throttle with his boat in the stream.

†Among the young members of the choir was Harold W. Castner, who would later become an author of local history in the Damariscotta area. Mr. Castner's histories have been very valuable in the preparation of this work.

Charter trips on *Anodyne* continued to be successful, but the 36-foot length of the boat was restrictive. On one charter for a fraternal organization's clambake at Prentis' Island, a large scow, *Juno*, was rigged with makeshift benches consisting of planks perched precariously on temporary uprights. I cannot help wondering about the discomfort and apprehension of the order's members as the diminutive *Anodyne* towed them two and a half miles downriver from Damariscotta.[12]

The 1900 operating season with *Anodyne* was a resounding success. The demand for steamboat service on the Damariscotta was growing with unanticipated vigor. Elliot Gamage was in the right place at the right time, and he had the right background to supply the transportation needs of the area. If anything, business was too good. Captain Gamage realized that he could not meet the demand, and that expansion of the fleet was necessary.

Proceeding with typical Yankee caution, Captain Gamage tested the waters by discussing his plans for expansion with several prominent citizens. Receiving enthusiastic support, Elliot P. Gamage formed the Damariscotta Steamboat Company in the fall of 1900.[13] Stock was offered at $25 per share and was quickly subscribed.[14] Captain Gamage served as manager of the new company while retaining his position as captain on the boat.[15]

The Damariscotta Steamboat Company immediately ordered a new steamer from the yards of A & M Gamage and Sons at Bristol. Named for the port at which she was built, the steamer *Bristol* had registered dimensions of 67.9' in length, 16.9' beam, and 6.2' depth with a gross tonnage of 48 and 21 net. She could carry more than a hundred passengers and required a crew of three in addition to the captain. She was awarded an official number of 3879. *Bristol* was launched in the spring of 1901.[16]

The Damariscotta Steamboat Company fleet before 1908 consisted of *Newcastle, Bristol,* and the diminutive *Anodyne.* (Postcard from the author's collection)

Damariscotta River Steamboat Co's fleet.

There are three main components to consider when building a steamboat: the hull, the engine, and the boiler. The decision to use the Gamage yard was a logical one, given that Elliot's father and uncle were the owners. When it came to the machinery, they decided to install an engine built by James H. Paine & Son.[17]

Paine was a Boston-based manufacturer who had been building stationary and marine steam engines since about 1874.[18] Paine engines were not strangers to Maine waters. They had been used in boats at Bangor, Bar Harbor, Portland, Rockland, Castine, and on the inland waters of Moosehead Lake.[19] The engine selected for

Bristol was a two-cylinder compound with piston valves.[20]

Although the Paine company claimed that "...our engines are as near perfect as is possible to make"[21] Captain Gamage did have some problems with the new power plant. Harold Castner reported that *Bristol*'s engine was prone to overheating* and that *Anodyne* frequently had to make the run as the substitute boat.[22]

---

*I suspect that the problem was overheating of the bearings, which is not uncommon to new engines. Once the connecting rods and the crankshaft worked in and the shims were set to the proper clearance such a problem would disappear.

The "Queen of the Fleet," the steamer *Newcastle* is shown at Poole's Landing. The framework to the left is for loading ice onto schooners during the important winter harvest. Note the semaphore on the right end of the dock to signal passing steamers when passengers were waiting to board. (Nobleboro Historical Society, Pictorial Studio)

Bristol replaced *Anodyne* on "the river route"[23] and the older boat began service on John's Bay.[24] *Bristol*'s first day of service was June 1, 1901.[25] Additional stops at Poole's Landing and Clarks Cove were added with two round trips scheduled during the busy summer months.[26] As Harold Castner states in his writing about the two boats, "It seemed certain that these two steamers could accommodate the demand, but in the very first year of 1901 it was found that the demand was far greater, and a much larger steamer was planned, approved, and built by the same Gamage yard in 1902." This new boat was the "Queen of the Fleet," the steamer *Newcastle*,[27] ordered in the fall of 1901. She was registered at 80' in length, with a 17.9' beam and a draft of 6.9'. Her gross tonnage was 83 with a net of 41. As an inland passenger steamer, she was required to carry a crew of four in addition to the captain. Her official number was 130963 in 1902. *Newcastle* is a classic example of a turn-of-the-century inland steamer.

The problems encountered with the engine in *Bristol* could not have been severe, because another Paine engine was installed in *Newcastle*. This was a two-cylinder "Class E" compound type that featured in-line cylinders of 10 and 20 inches diameter with a stroke of 14. It had piston valves located between the two cylinders, which permitted the engine to be placed with the low-pressure cylinder close to the engineroom bulkhead. This allowed an important saving of space in a small passenger steamer.

Newcastle's engine was ordered with larger main journals and crank pins than those in *Bristol*. This supports the theory that the overheating problem in *Bristol* was in the bearings. *Newcastle*'s engine had Stephenson link valve gear that was hand-operated by a lever in the center of the engine. The engine was over seven feet tall, with a length of about six feet. It weighed 5,500 pounds.[28]

As the launch date for *Newcastle* approached, the details of the ceremony became a topic at the directors' meeting. Director John L. Clifford suggested that the youngest stockholder be the sponsor for the new steamer. The board approved the suggestion and a search of company records revealed that young Harold W. Castner held one share of stock. This was enough to qualify him and the 13-year-old stockholder was given the honor.[29]

Investment in the steamboat company had been well-supported by the citizens of Damariscotta and Newcastle. Significant among them were a number of influential women of the community. With the temperance movement in Maine at its strongest these zealots of sobriety insisted that the boat not be christened with the traditional bottle of champagne. The fact that the sponsor was a mere boy lended support to this position. Seizing control of the plans for the ceremony, the ladies prepared an appropriate bottle with which to send the vessel down the ways. On the morning of the launching the self-appointed committee gathered on the dock at the bow of *Newcastle* and prompted the young sponsor on the speech they had prepared for him. "All were in a state of 'jitters' awaiting the great event."[30]

While the shipyard's launch crew made their final preparations, a vibration on the boat caused the nervous ladies to jump into action prematurely. At their insistence, young Harold recited the words, "I christen thee good ship *Newcastle*, and may good luck go with thee forever." He swung the bottle in a great arc, successfully shattering it on the stem in a most professional manner. Unfortunately, Captain Plummer Leeman was at his post on the jackscrew directly under the bow. The premature baptism succeeded in christening the good captain as well as the boat.

The new steamer shuddered momentarily; then, gaining momentum, slid gracefully into the waters of

The Maine Central Railroad station at Newcastle was the disembarcation point for many summer visitors to the Damariscotta River region. Steamboats were scheduled to arrive at Damariscotta-Newcastle with ample time for passengers to walk the half-mile to or from the railroad depot. (Nobleboro Historical Society, Pictorial Studio)

the Damariscotta River. It appears that Captain Leeman was not only surprised by the event but was also curious as to why the distinct odor of alcohol had not yet emanated from his clothing. He came to the dock inquiring of the ladies what was in the bottle. Castner reports that, "The ladies, in no uncertain terms, informed him that it was pure water. The captain was a most congenial and pleasant man and was laughing about the whole affair, but the ladies were deadly in earnest."[31]

Newcastle made her inaugural run on June 1, 1902.[32] She was an imposing vessel for the small river, admired by all. And with *Newcastle* serving the river route, *Bristol* became an excursion boat to Monhegan and other points along the coast. In 1903, *Newcastle* was leased by the U.S. government and left Damariscotta in the spring. Captain Plummer Leeman and his son Elliot ran the boat all that summer in Portland for the U.S. Army's Quartermaster Department. Their mission was to support the forts in Portland Harbor and Casco Bay by providing transportation for troops and supplies to the island outposts. This was a profitable arrangement that resulted in generous dividends for the stockholders. *Newcastle* returned in late fall and operated on the Damariscotta for the next four years.[33]

When *Newcastle* and *Bristol* were both in service, Captain Elliot Gamage commanded *Newcastle* while Captain Leeman served as master of *Bristol*.[34] Uncle Charlie Hatch was engineer on the boats and was most often found on *Newcastle*. His son Warren was in charge of the engineroom in *Bristol*.[35] As Harold Castner reminisced, "We can still remember his immaculate engine room and those great pistons and shiny engine parts, and the lovable countenance of Uncle Charlie looking up at us."[36]

By the fall of 1903, the Damariscotta Steamboat Company had been awarded a mail contract.[37] The terms of this lucrative agreement required service throughout the year. Cold temperatures and the resulting ice made many waterways this far north impassable during winter months. However, the lower freezing temperature of salt water, strong currents, and the nine-foot rise and fall of the tide kept the Damariscotta River open to navigation during all but the most extreme months of the New England winters.

This year-round operation of the steamboats also had a positive impact on the lives of the student population of the Damariscotta River valley. Each village along the river had a one-room schoolhouse where local children received the rudiments of education. When they reached secondary-school age, the students would travel to Newcastle to attend classes at Lincoln Academy. To reach the Academy, young scholars would walk the dirt roads to the town at the head of the river. During winter months snow made travel difficult. The ensuing mud season reduced the land to an non-navigable quagmire. When the roads were impassable, students were forced to stay in boarding houses near the school, an arrangement enjoyed by few. Year-round operation of the boats provided not only reliable transportation but also the warmth of a coal fire during the coldest days. The engineroom became a popular spot on these daily trips through the waters of winter.* The undulating machinery mesmerized many a young passenger and provided the impetus for some to follow a

---

*Historian Nicholas Dean gave this account of traveling to school in the winter to me during my visit to Maine in November 1994. Nick has provided me with valuable information and insight throughout the preparation of this document, for which I am most grateful.

career in marine engineering.

The steamer would lie over at Damariscotta on Saturday night and Sunday. She would bunker at the coal shed of Thomas E. Gay across the river in Newcastle[38] and be ready for her first trip downriver Monday morning.

Bristol had enjoyed only a brief moment in the spotlight of the Damariscotta Steamboat Company when she was upstaged by "The Queen of the Fleet," *Newcastle*, in 1902. With *Newcastle* as the star of the show, *Bristol* was relegated to the less-prestigious position of "second boat." Her decline in stature is documented in the *Merchant Vessel Lists. Bristol* was maintained as an inland passenger vessel from 1901 through 1905.

Subsequently, she was listed as a towboat, a status maintained for the next three years.

The year 1908 was a significant year for the Damariscotta Steamboat Company. *Newcastle* was again leased by the U.S. government[39] for service in Portland, this time attached to the Engineering Department at Casco Bay.[40] In addition to the lease, the steamboat company decided to expand its operations by building another steamer for service at the south end of the river. The most significant change in the fortunes of the Damariscotta Steamboat Company, however, went unnoticed by the principals of the company. In October 1908 the first Model "T" rolled out of the Ford plant in Detroit.[41] Transportation would never again be the same.

Fort William Henry provides an imposing backdrop for this photograph of *Tourist* at Pemaquid Beach. (Allie Ryan Maritime Collection, courtesy of Maine State Museum, Augusta, Maine)

CHAPTER 3

ANOTHER NEW BOAT

AFTER SEVEN YEARS OF operation, the Damariscotta Steamboat Company was enjoying a thriving business with no end in sight. With the 1908 season on the horizon, Elliot P. Gamage had secured a U.S. government lease for *Newcastle* to work in Portland for the summer. This left *Bristol* as the largest and principal boat on the line, with two daily trips required from the landing at the Damariscotta-Newcastle bridge to the southern extremity of the river. Passengers could disembark at Christmas Cove or at any of several stops en route. Once at the "Cove," they could transfer to the Damariscotta Steamboat Company's smaller boat and continue to one of the lesser landings in John's Bay.

Small steamboats that made connections with larger vessels and ferried passengers and freight to ancillary landings were known as annex boats. The annex boat for the Damariscotta Steamboat Company at this time was *Anodyne*. The company scheduled the 13-year-old veteran to make ten circuits of the bay each day.[1] Although *Anodyne* had served nobly during the formative years of the company, the increase in demand for steamboat travel caused ridership to outgrow the capacity of the 36' former liniment carrier. Anticipating a demanding season for 1908, the board of the Damariscotta Steamboat Company decided to build another boat.

The choice of a shipbuilder for the first two Damariscotta steamers had been a simple one – the A&M Gamage shipyard at East Boothbay. Captain Elliot P. Gamage's uncle, Albion, and his father, Menzies, had ensured that *Newcastle* and *Bristol* were of top quality. However, when it came time to build a new annex boat, the A&M Gamage yard was closed. In fact, the 1902 steamer *Newcastle* was the last vessel built by the yard.[2]

The February 15, 1908, edition of the *Boothbay Register* reported that the W. Irving Adams and Son shipyard at East Boothbay had "...contracted to build a fine little steamboat, fifty-five feet long, for the Damariscotta Steamboat Company."[3] The Adams family had been building vessels for generations. W. Irving's father, William, and uncle, Andrew, engaged in the shipbuilding business first in North Boothbay's Ovens Mouth River and later in East Boothbay.[4] When the partnership A&W Adams dissolved in 1857, W. Irving became a part-

The James H. Paine and Son machine shop at Noank, Connecticut, where *Tourist*'s engine was manufactured. *Sabino* (ex-*Tourist*) steams past this site each night on her downriver cruise from Mystic Seaport. (Noank Historical Society)

ner with his father.[5] William (senior) died in 1891, and William Irving continued the business as W. Irving Adams and Son. In July 1904, William Irving Adams and his son, Frank C., celebrated the launching of their one-hundredth vessel.[6]

W. Irving Adams & Son launched many fine sailing vessels, including the four-masted schooner *Eleanor F. Bartram* for Captain Benjamin E. Pinkham of Boothbay Harbor.[7] As the twentieth century progressed, the yard produced an increasing number of steamers. The building time for a schooner was nearly a year, but a steamboat took only about three months.

On January 2, 1908, the Adams yard laid the keel for an 88' passenger steamer. On April 14, the new boat was christened *Islander*. The *Boothbay Register* for that week reported that "The launching was the 120th to take place from the yard of the veteran East Boothbay shipbuilders and was a success in every way."[8]

The next boat scheduled for launching from the Adams yard was the steamer being built for the Damariscotta Steamboat Company. On May 7, 1908, the little steamer slid into the waters of the Damariscotta River and was christened *Tourist*.[9] Only eleven weeks had elapsed since the contract had been awarded. To the uninitiated, a launching, with all its ceremony and jubilation, may seem like the end of the shipbuilding process and the beginning of the steaming career of the vessel. This, however, is not the case. Hulls are launched bare and empty. They must undergo extensive work on rigging, machinery installation, and myriad other details before delivery to the owner.

Two days after the launching of hull 121,[10] the *Boothbay Register* reported, "Our genial Capt. Elliot Gamage of the Damariscotta Steamboat line has been in town this week superintending the final touches to the new boat which was launched Thursday from W. I. Adams yard. She is a little beauty and is named the '*Tourist*.' The sloop 'Jumbo Begious' arrived Thursday and will be used to put in the boiler and engine in the steamer '*Tourist*.'"[11]

Tourist's boiler was a watertube type, designed and built by Murray & Tregurtha of Boston.[12] This class of boiler was constructed of wrought iron pipe with malleable iron elbows and unions. The boiler featured two rows of large-diameter wrought iron side pipes, one row on each side of the grates. A series of circulating pipes extended over the fire from each side pipe. This design provided for a large heating surface within a relatively small boiler casing.[13] This was a very efficient type of boiler and one that was well suited for a small steamboat such as *Tourist*.

The boiler installed in *Tourist* was three years old.[14] It is most likely that this boiler had been used in another boat, as most companies made each boiler to order. A new boiler of the size needed for *Tourist* cost about $1,000 in 1908.[15] It seems that the frugal Captain Gamage was trying to save a few dollars in the construction of his new boat.

Evidently the performance of the engines in *Bristol* and *Newcastle* pleased the directors of the steamboat company. They ordered another Paine compound engine for *Tourist*. This engine was a smaller version of the "Class E" engine installed in *Newcastle*. The new engine had a high-pressure cylinder diameter of seven inches and a low-pressure cylinder diameter of fourteen with a common stroke of twelve. The engine developed 80 indicated horsepower.[16]

Boston was the home of James H. Paine & Son when they manufactured the engines for *Bristol* and *Newcastle*. In 1903, the company moved to Noank, Connecticut,[17]

The Paine "Class E" compound steam engine. This is an illustration of the engine installed in the steamer *Newcastle*. It is the same class as the engine in *Sabino*. Those who are familiar with *Sabino*'s engine will notice the absence of tail rods protruding from the upper heads. (Noank Historical Society)

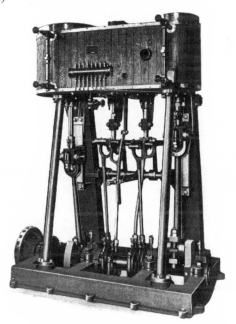

and located in Palmer's middle shipyard on the Mystic River.* Here they remained as James H. Paine & Son, Inc. until June 1908,[18] when the name was changed to the New England Marine Engine Company.[†]

---

*This information came as a result of my interview with Robert Palmer at the Noank Historical Society in 1991. There were two interviews, the second of which was audiotaped by the historical society.

[†]The New England Marine Engine Company continued to advertise as a steam-engine manufacturer, but ventured into the emerging gasoline-engine field. Their design of a two-cylinder, two-stroke engine more closely resembled a steam engine than gasoline engines of the day. The enterprise failed and the New England Marine Engine Company slipped into oblivion, but not before leaving us with one engine design improvement. In their advertisements of 1909, the New England Marine Engine Company boasted of "A SLEEVE in the cylinders, never before used, REVOLUTIONIZED engine building. A patent is pending." Cylinder sleeves were a significant improvement and are common today in both gasoline and diesel engines.

The construction of the engine for *Tourist* is clearly documented in the pages of the *New London Day*. The first reference, dated February 10, 1908, reads, "The J. H. Paine & Son Machine Co. of this place has signed a contract for the construction of a marine steam engine for the Damariscotta Steamboat Company of Maine to be installed in a new boat being built in *Boston* [sic] to run between South Bristol and *New Castle*, [sic] Maine. The engine will be a 7 - 14 x 12 regular Paine engine."[19]

By February 25, the castings for the engine had arrived in Noank and a "large force of men" was working full time to finish the engine.[20] The fact that the castings "had arrived" gives support to the theory that the Paine Company's foundry work was still done in Boston and that the machine work and assembly were done in Noank. The completed engine was loaded on a freight car on the morning of May 2, and "Shipped to its owner E.P. Gamage, South Bristol, Maine." The *New London*

Tourist running astern at Cotrell's Wharf in Damariscotta with her lines made fast. This procedure is still followed today. The purpose is to heat the engine thoroughly before getting underway. This image shows *Tourist* as she looked in 1908-09. (Postcard from the author's collection)

Day's report goes on to say that "The engine is a regular style of Paine engine and is 7 by 14 by 12 and is 100 horsepower. It is to be used as a passenger steamer running on the Damariscotta River between South Bristol and East Boothbay."[21]

The *Day*'s report on the engine gives the horsepower as one hundred. The first horsepower listed in the *List of Merchant Vessels* is 80; later it is listed as 75. This is not as inconsistent as it might first appear. The one-hundred-horsepower rating is what we consider "nominal horsepower." This term, originated by James Watt, is the power that an engine will develop calculated from its cylinder diameter.[22] Engine builders and purchasers use this calculated power when discussing the various sizes of engines. It can best be thought of as a rough guess of the vessel's needs and the theoretical output of the engine.[23]

The horsepower rating of 80 in the *List of Merchant Vessels* is "indicated horsepower."* This value is much more accurate as it is a true measure of the work being done within the cylinders of the steam engine, ". . . and is based upon no assumptions, but is actually calculated."[24] The change in indicated horsepower from 80 to 75 simply reflects a change in either engine speed or, more likely, the pressure in the boiler. The allowable working pressure of a boiler is often reduced as the pressure vessel increases in age. A reduction in pressure of only six

East Boothbay, Maine. Glimpse of the East Boothbay Ship Yards.

W. Irving Adams' shipyard at East Boothbay, where *Tourist* was built in eleven weeks. (Postcard from the author's collection)

pounds per square inch would result in a decrease of five horsepower in this engine.

On May 14, 1908, Elliot P. Gamage made application for an official number to the Collector of Customs in the district of Waldoboro, Maine. He listed *Tourist*'s homeport as Damariscotta and signed the document as the vessel's master. The vessel is described as a single-deck, screw steamer of 24 gross tons and 9 net. Her registered dimensions are 45.2' length, 15.3' beam, and 5.4' depth.[25]

There has been a great deal of controversy about *Tourist*'s length. There are those who have written that she was lengthened at some point during her career. In fact, three different owners are credited with an extension of the hull that I contend never occurred.

---

*Indicated horsepower is calculated from the average pressure acting on the piston throughout the entire length of the stroke. A device called an engine indicator measures this pressure. The indicator is mechanically attached to the engine and produces a graphical representation of the events occurring within the cylinder. The graph shows changes in pressure and volume as the engine runs. By measuring the area of the graph, the engineer can calculate the mean pressure acting on the piston. This figure is then combined with piston area, length of stroke, and the number of power strokes per minute to arrive at the indicated horsepower.

The registered length of a vessel of this type is measured from the fore part of the outer planking on the side of the stem to the after part of the main sternpost.[26] The admeasurement document for *Tourist* lists the registered length as 45.2'. This document also contains the figures used to arrive at the various lengths, breadths, and tonnages contained therein. Using the figures contained in the document, the registered length is actually calculated to be 51.75'.* This is within one inch of the actual measurement of *Sabino* today. The unmeasured space aft of the rudderpost is 5.1' plus an unmeasured stem width of 0.6 feet, for an overall length of 57.45'. This is within four inches of the current overall length of the boat.

Tourist was awarded an official number of 205213. As a vessel under ten tons, she was required to carry a crew of two in addition to the master.[27] These two crew members would have been an engineer and a deckhand.

As the new boat was prepared for its entrance into the service of the Damariscotta Steamboat Company, the first steamer built for the line was sold to the State of New York to be used as a prison boat for Sing Sing.[28] *Bristol*'s departure did not go unnoticed by the local press. "Steamer *Bristol* was into Pierces & Hartung's Thursday morning coaling up on her way to Port Chester, N.Y., where she has been sold by the Damariscotta Steamboat Company..." The article went on to report that *Tourist* would be the replacement boat for the local company.[29]

The initial inspection of *Tourist* was held on June 2, 1908, at Damariscotta.[†] A Steamboat-Inspection Service officer for the local district of Bangor examined the hull and the machinery and issued a certificate of inspection as an "Inland Passenger Steamer."[30] *Tourist* embarked on her career as a passenger steamer on the following day, June 3. She replaced *Newcastle* on the river route long enough to have the larger boat "painted up fine for the summer season."[31]

The general public was eager to see the trim new vessel of the Damariscotta fleet. On June 4, she was open for inspection: ". . . and won instant public acceptance."[32] The *Lincoln County News* had the following report. "The new boat, the "*Tourist*," came up river for the first time, it is a snug little craft and is a credit to the company."[33]

Advertisements in the local paper announced that *Tourist* would start running on the John's Bay route on June 25.[34] This route, previously served by *Anodyne*, included landings at South Bristol, Pemaquid Beach, Pemaquid Point, Christmas Cove, and Heron Island. *Newcastle* served the river route terminating at Christmas Cove, where passengers would transfer to the annex boat for the landings in John's Bay.

On June 30, the new boat made its first appearance in Boothbay Harbor. The event was recorded in the pages of the *Boothbay Register*. "The steamer *Tourist*, just completed by W. Irving Adams & Son, for the Damariscotta

---

*I cannot state with certainty why there is a discrepancy of more than 6' in the registered length as recorded and the registered length as calculated. I can state that the shorter registered length was an advantage to the owner in that it would result in a lower registered tonnage. Tonnage, which is a measurement of volume and not weight, is the basis for taxes and manning requirements of a vessel. *Tourist* had a gross tonnage of just less than 25 tons and a net tonnage of 9. Slightly larger tonnages would have resulted in higher fees and the need for a larger crew.

---

†It is interesting to note that the inspection date is less than four weeks from her launch date and only four months from the date the construction contract was signed.

Steamboat Landing, Pemaquid Beach, Me.

The Pemaquid Point landing with *Tourist* in her original configuration. Due to its exposure to the ocean, landings were made here "…only at the discretion of the captain." (Allie Ryan Maritime Collection, courtesy of Maine State Museum, Augusta, Maine)

Meeting the noon boat at Christmas Cove was a social event. Visitors and residents alike scurried to make connections and meet guests. Those without specific duties just came down to watch. (Pictorial Supplement of the *Christmas Cove Improvement Association Notes*, courtesy of Mansfield Hunt)

Captain Alfred Harrington collects the 35¢ round-trip fare on the upper deck of the steamer *Tourist*. (*Pictorial Supplement* of the *Christmas Cove Improvement Association Notes*, courtesy of Mansfield Hunt)

Steamboat Co. was in the harbor Tuesday to coal up at Pierce & Hartung's and many of our citizens looked her over. She is a fine little craft, just what the company needs for an annex boat for South Bristol."[55]

Tourist lay overnight at South Bristol. Her location in this picturesque harbor is documented in postcards and photographs of the period. Each morning at 5:45 she would begin her rounds of Pemaquid, Christmas Cove and South Bristol.[36] The landing at Pemaquid Beach was just west of Fort William Henry. This defensive outpost, which predates *Tourist* by two hundred years, continues to be a popular attraction for visitors today. One of the earliest known photographs of *Tourist* was taken at this landing. This photo, later made into a postcard, shows *Tourist* at the steamer landing with the imposing fort standing invincibly in the background.

It may seem redundant to establish a landing at Pemaquid Harbor since it is only 300 yards across the river from Pemaquid Beach. However, to walk from one landing to the other would require two hours of vigorous hiking. For those with better things to do, the Damariscotta Steamboat Company offered an expeditious alternative, as the little steamer could scoot across from one landing to the other in about two minutes. There are few who remember the landing at Pemaquid Point, which leads me to believe that it was a short-lived point of embarkation. This promontory is the farthest-reaching point into the Atlantic on the eastern shore of the river. As such, it can boast of challenging sea conditions, regularly testing both vessel and crew. With tragic regularity unwary visitors to the point are still swept from the rocks into the frigid waters of the Atlantic.

A 1912 schedule for *Tourist* documents contemporary concerns about conditions at Pemaquid Point. "Landings at Pemaquid Point on account of its exposed position will be made only at the discretion of the Captain."[57] One recollection of the landing at the point provides the following insight:

> On a rough day, it was an experience to ride on the *Tourist*. She left the Cove from a big float just south of Bar Cottage, and she crossed the bay to an immense pontoon dock at Pemaquid Point, somewhere north of the lighthouse but within walking distance thereof. In anything like a good sailing breeze, its antics were spectacular. So were those of the little steamers. Captain Harrington had authority to land, or to refrain from landing, at discretion. He rarely refrained, but not many of us would dare to do the same. Any wind with west in it makes it a lee shore, a minor miscalculation, and the ship would hit the rocks.[58]

The steamer landing at Christmas Cove was a popular spot and a center of social activity. Before the days of television and video games, the entertainment of choice was to run to the steamer landing whenever a whistle announced the boat's arrival.[39] There were four landings a day for *Tourist* and two for *Newcastle*. Additionally, boats of the Eastern Steamship Company and the Bristol Navigation Company made daily visits to the Cove. These activities at the dock kept many young visitors busy all day.

The art of docking a steamboat was appreciated in its day, and onlookers compared the skills of various captains. The boat would approach to about two feet from the dock and a spring line would be sent over. The captain would ring full speed astern and the water would be churned into foam as the boat trembled to a stop. There were no paid line-handlers in those days but there was always someone who would take a mooring line from the deckhand. Boys would scramble for the prestige of

Tourist at Boothbay Harbor. The head, constructed aft of the ladies' cabin, and the pilothouse searchlight date this image after 1915. Although the steamer is buttoned up for the winter, the sailing vessel in the background is rigged and ready to go. (Allie Ryan Maritime Collection, courtesy of Maine State Museum, Augusta, Maine)

November 1910 saw snow in the Damariscotta River valley. Here Rear Admiral William F. Royall, U.S.N (Ret.), stands close to his mother as the family, servant, and crew pose to capture a moment in time. The occasion was a special trip on *Tourist* that began the family's winter pilgrimage from East Boothbay to Bermuda. (Photo courtesy of Rear Admiral Royall)

being the one who caught the line and aided the captain in another successful landing.

Once the lines were fast, the boat could be held tightly against the dock by running the engine slowly ahead to keep tension on the spring line. To depart, the captain would ring slow astern and the boat would swing out from the dock. One bell for stop and another for ahead and *Tourist* would be underway again on her familiar circuit of John's Bay.[40]

Once a boat landed, Lewis Thorpe would load the baggage into his waiting wagon[41] and deliver it to any of the ten hotels and boarding houses for which it was destined.[42] It seems that no matter which hostelry had been chosen Mr. Thorpe was able to get the luggage there before its owner arrived.

The crews of *Tourist, Newcastle,* and Bristol Navigation Company's *Islesford* were the most popular among the local residents. Those of Eastern Steamship's "Bath Boat" were regarded as "a trifle unfriendly."[43] The former boats were smaller and locally owned. I suspect it was somewhat like knowing the driver of the local bus while the operator of the interstate Greyhound remains a busy and aloof stranger.

Tourist and the other boats would stop at private landings on request. One such landing was that of the Royall family at East Boothbay. There is a historic photograph of the Royall family standing on the deck of *Tourist* in November 1910 in which Rear Admiral William F. Royall, U.S. Navy (Retired), age six at the time, is seen holding his mother's hand. The occasion was the family's departure from East Boothbay for their winter retreat to Bermuda. They would depart on *Tourist* for the short trip to Damariscotta-Newcastle, from which point they would take the train to New York City. From there they would board a steamship for southern waters.[44]

A steamboat, like any other mechanical contrivance, is subject to occasional breakdowns. To minimize disruptions in service, the engineer is responsible for anticipating potential problems and addressing them before a breakdown occurs. Often, the effectiveness of an engineer is measured by his success in the mystical art of foreseeing these problems. Some engineroom accouterments give ample warning, and if the symptoms are observed, application of corrective measures in sufficient time can avert catastrophe. On other occasions, the malady manifests itself with a suddenness that punctuates an otherwise boring day with a moment of stark terror. In marine engineering there is no such thing as a pleasant surprise.

One component of the propulsion system that warrants special consideration and respectful attentiveness is the steam boiler. This device has deservingly earned a reputation as the most lethal component of steamboating. Boilers for compound engines, such as *Tourist's*, operate in the range of 150 to 180 pounds per square inch of steam pressure. If released suddenly by an explosion, not only does the force destroy the surrounding structure and people, but the water contained within the boiler flashes into steam that scalds everything and everyone it touches. This potential devastation causes engineers to pay special attention to the condition and operation of their boilers.

By 1913, the boiler in *Tourist* was eight years old. Although this is not old age for a boiler, the engineer felt that it had reached a point where replacement was the prudent course. A new boiler was ordered from Bath Iron Works[45] at Bath, Maine, and installed in *Tourist* prior to June 14, 1913.[46]

Boiler problems were not the only tribulations faced by those engaged in the steamboat trade. The *Boothbay Register* reported an especially bad week shortly after *Tourist* received her new boiler. "The steamer *Tourist* has

The crew of the steamer *Newcastle* could be found on any of the Damariscotta Steamboat Company's vessels depending on the needs and schedule of service. From left to right they are: Charles Foster, Everett Leighton, Horace Kelsey, Floyd McFarland, Engineer Charles Hatch, and Captain Elliot P. Gamage. (Harold Castner collection, courtesy of Skidompha Public Library)

had troubles this past week, troubles which, while not serious, were at least exasperating and caused a break in her scheduled trips. On Wednesday, while passing through the drawbridge the guy of the derrick used in hoisting the debris from the blasting operation in the gut struck the smoke stack and broke it off. This was soon repaired and after missing one or two trips she was on her route again. Later the staunch little steamer had to lay off and go to Boothbay Harbor to have her low-pressure cylinder bored out."[47] Although the details of the problem in the low-pressure cylinder are not recorded in the *Register*, this is the type of repair that would be necessary following the breaking of a piston ring or similar surprise.

Tourist and other steamers of the period provided a great variety of services to river communities. The name *Tourist* seems to imply that the duties of the little steamer were limited to delivering summer visitors to and from their accommodations. This was not the case, and perhaps explains why one newspaper reported her arrival on the river with the quotation, "She's a peach, all but her name."[48] Transporting vacationers was but one service provided by the steamer. Of more significance to the permanent residents was the fact that *Tourist* was the mail boat. When she was running, there were a total of three mail deliveries each day–one by wagon and two by steamboat. When winter's ice prevented river navigation, the only mail reaching downriver communities arrived by wagon or sleigh. During the summer months, when *Tourist* was on the John's Bay route, *Newcastle* provided the mail service.

Newcastle was nearly twice the size of *Tourist*. She required a larger crew and consumed more fuel than her diminutive counterpart. Due to the cost of operation, *Newcastle* was scheduled to run only during the peak of the summer season when large numbers of visitors arrived for their vacations. During the rest of the year, *Tourist* provided service on the river route.

The Damariscotta Steamboat Company operated *Tourist* as long into the winter as the weather would allow. The advertised schedule was from March through December.[49] This was an ambitious goal and one that was often unachievable. Reports of delayed service due to ice on the river frequently appeared in the local papers during *Tourist*'s Damariscotta career.*

It is difficult for us – everyday users of today's extraordinary transportation and communications resources–to appreciate the profound isolation experienced by coastal residents during the long Maine winters. For many, the only link with the outside world was provided by the steamboat company. The elation of the winter-weary residents is noted in the March 28, 1914, edition of the *Boothbay Register* with the following quote: "The regular trips of the Damariscotta boat are cordially welcomed. We feel nearer to somewhere."[50]

Tourist proved to be a versatile little steamer and provided a variety of services to a great many people. Her uncomplicated design suited the simple needs of her clientele and the simplicity of the work she did. The choices a naval architect makes in designing a vessel are circumscribed by several factors. Paramount among these is the intended use of the boat. Other factors, such as navigational limitations, government regulations, and docking facilities, need to be taken into account early in the planning stages.

In her original design, *Tourist* was an unpretentious little steamer and the smallest boat built for the Damariscotta Steamboat Company. Despite her diminu-

---

*There are many reports in the *Boothbay Register* of *Tourist* being delayed by ice in the river. One of the latest was a report of the steamer being "turned back by a flow of ice" on April 4, 1914.

tive size, she had a small crew's quarters below the pilot-house extending under the foredeck. The crew space was 18' long and had limited headroom with standing room only in the center of the compartment.[51] There was a small stove on the starboard side with a chimney, or "Charlie Noble," extending a short distance above the main deck. Photos from the period show smoke stains on the pilothouse from the galley stove.

Access to the crew's quarters was on the starboard side. A door was tucked under the overhang of the upper deck at the rear of the pilothouse. This entrance from the main deck led down a few steps to the small compartment. On the port side, opposite the door, was a window through which curious passengers could survey the private sanctuary. Two additional windows were located

inches above the main deck just forward of each door to the pilothouse. A galley space was under the pilothouse on the starboard side. The deckhand was the designated cook.[52] The culinary delights prepared in the modest galley have not been documented, but it would be safe to assume that a pot of coffee was always at the ready.

The deck of the pilothouse was approximately four feet above the main deck. There were four steps reaching up to the pilothouse on the port side. There was also a door on the starboard side of the pilothouse but there were no steps because of the stack for the galley stove. This resulted in a somewhat unbalanced look to the pilothouse. The space below the pilothouse provided headroom in the crew space below.

The main deck extended some twelve feet forward

LaForest Etheridge purchased the Damariscotta Steamboat Company in 1917. In the winter months he met the requirements of his mail contract by making deliveries to the Round Pond post office in his pung. Notice the wood stove chimney protruding from the roof. (Nobleboro Historical Society, Pictorial Studio)

from the pilothouse to the stem. Passengers were allowed to stand on the open deck, as they were well below the level of the pilothouse windows and thus posed no encumbrance to the captain's view of the river.

The lady's cabin or saloon (pronounced the same as a drinking establishment in the Old West) was a feature of note from the start. One newspaper account of *Tourist*'s initial open house on June 4, 1908, had nothing but praise for this space. The popularity of the cabin was still of interest to the press some 19 years later when the *Portland Press Herald* noted that "...there is a separate saloon for the ladies."[55]

The superstructure aft of the pilothouse enclosed the engineroom and the lady's saloon. Access to the engineroom was through doors on either side of the super-structure. There was a window on each side of the engineroom between the door and the bulkhead separating the engineering spaces and the crew's quarters. A second window was located on each side, aft of the door. *Tourist* most often operated with these doors and windows open, since there were no ventilators to bring fresh air down to the engineer.

The stairway to the upper deck ran athwartships from the port side. The treads and risers of the stairs were attached directly to the after bulkhead of the engineroom. The outline of these steps can still be seen on the boat today.

Despite the forethought that goes into each design feature, changes in a vessel's service often dictate a modification of the original configuration. *Tourist* was designed

LaForest Etheridge expanded his transportation interests when he bought a used car. The vehicle was a 1905 Buick Model C with a two-cylinder engine and electric headlights. Etheridge used the five-passenger touring car to deliver mail and carry passengers for hire in competition with the steamboats. (Nobleboro Historical Society, Pictorial Studio)

as the annex boat for John's Bay. Within a few years of her launching, her duties expanded to include service on the river route during the spring and fall seasons. This increase in her scope of operation necessitated alterations to her original design.

In announcing *Tourist*'s debut on the river for 1915, the *Boothbay Register* provides us with some details of a structural change. "The steamer *Tourist* expects to resume her daily trips to Damariscotta on Monday. This steamer has been fitted with an addition to its cabin giving it increased accommodations."[54] The addition referred to in the newspaper was an extension of the ladies saloon that took it aft to the rail. It appears that there was a toilet included in this area, as a water tank appears on the starboard side of the cabin top with this modification. The addition of such a convenience would certainly be appreciated by passengers and crew on the two-hour trips from Damariscotta to Christmas Cove.

With the changes to the saloon came changes to the upper deck. A permanent, fixed canopy was constructed over the upper deck. This replaced a very temporary-looking canvas awning rigged to provide cover during the summer months. The small boat, which had hung from davits on the upper deck, was raised to a cradle on top of the canopy.

Another change made late in the 1915 season reflects *Tourist*'s extended operating hours. The October 22 edition of the *Boothbay Register* reports that the little steamer had been fitted with a spotlight.[55] It appears that the electricity for the spotlight came from a small steam turbine-generator similar to those used on locomotives. Lights on the steamer would have been 32 volts, in keeping with the marine practice of the period. A steam turbine remains on the boat today. The present installation is configured to charge 12-volt batteries, but an older 32-volt generator is still attached to the turbine.

The steamboat business started to change about the time *Tourist* entered the waters of the Damariscotta for the first time. In that year of 1908, 63,500 automobiles and 1,500 trucks and buses rolled out of American manufacturing plants. That was fifteen times the number of vehicles produced in 1900, the founding year of the Damariscotta Steamboat Company.[56] To add to the steamboater's problems, Henry Ford began production of his ubiquitous Model T in 1908, and in their first production year 10,067 cars were sold.[57]

By 1913, the Ford Motor Company was producing 1,000 cars per day.[58] By this time the popularity and affordability of privately-owned automobiles was having a severe impact on the small steamboat companies in Maine. No longer did visitors have to rely on the little steamers to get them from the depot to the hotel – they could drive there themselves. In fact, who needed to ride the train at all? More and more visitors chose to drive Down East on their own schedules rather than planning their vacations around the timetable of the Maine Central Railroad.

In an attempt to stay current in the changing world of public transport, Elliot P. Gamage purchased an "automobile truck" for the steamboat company in 1916.[59] He intended to use it to transfer baggage from the railroad station at *Newcastle* to the steamer landing at Damariscotta. This improvement in service did little to boost the sagging steamboat business.

By 1917, the mobilization of the masses had progressed to a point where the Damariscotta Steamboat Company could no longer effectively compete. Following the 1917 summer season, the directors of the company met and voted to cease operations.

On October 31, 1917, the Damariscotta Steamboat Company changed hands. Kendall M. Dunbar, legal counsel for the company, made an inventory of the assets. Captain LaForest "Foss" Etheridge purchased all rights and property, including *Tourist*. Captain Etheridge and Captain Mark Thompson became co-owners of Cotrell's Wharf in Damariscotta.[60] Captain Etheridge continued operation of steamboat service but changed the name of the company to the Damariscotta Steamboat Line,[61] while Captain Thompson operated a gasoline-powered boat from South Bristol to Cotrell's Wharf.

Foss Etheridge planned to operate the steamboat during the busy summer months and to fulfill the year-round obligations of the mail contract through the use of surface transportation. During the fair-weather months he would drive his 1905 Buick Model C touring car. In the winter, Foss's sleigh was the transport of choice. Being a clever Yankee, he had rigged a wood stove in the enclosed pung to ensure a comfortable ride for all passengers. It is reported that his was the most popular conveyance to South Bristol and Round Pond from the up-river communities.

In 1918, the *Boothbay Register* reported the first run of *Tourist* as occurring on June 1. The article also noted that "[S]he is now bringing noon and afternoon mail."[62]

Ten years after her launching, *Tourist* was the solitary steamboat flying the flag of the Damariscotta Steamboat Line. True, she had been elevated from the ancillary position of annex boat to the principal vessel of the company, but being the capital ship in a fleet of one is a hollow status indeed. Gasoline-powered land vehicles had been joined by gasoline-powered boats to encroach further into the territory of the steamboat. Captain Mark Thompson was running a gas boat from the same landing in Damariscotta that had been home to *Anodyne*, *Bristol*, and *Newcastle*. Even Plummer Leeman, who had been a Damariscotta River steamboat captain for years, exchanged his steamer *Islesford* for the gasoline-powered *George Popham* in June of that same year.[63]

Times were again changing and the changes did not favor the steamboat men.

Steamer „Newcastle" and Bridge, Damariscotta, Maine.   213949

The steamer *Newcastle* is shown here at the Damariscotta landing. Note the proximity to the bridge connecting the towns of Newcastle and Damariscotta. (Postcard from the author's collection)

CHAPTER 4

THE ACCIDENT

WHEN *TOURIST* WAS BUILT IN 1908 she was outfitted with a steam boiler and engine as previously described. As a vessel "...propelled in whole or part by steam" she was deemed a "steam vessel" within the regulations of the U.S. Steamboat Inspection Service.[1] Although this statement may seem blatantly obvious, a 1910 law created a re-definition of power vessels that would defy this logic.

On July 9, 1910, a law known colloquially as the "Motor Boat Act" went into effect. This law defines a motor boat as "...every vessel propelled by machinery and not more than sixty-five feet in length, except tug boats and tow boats propelled by steam."[2]

The law goes on to state, "...no such boat while so carrying passengers for hire shall be operated or navigated except in charge of a person duly licensed for such service by the local board of [Steamboat Inspection Service] inspectors. No examination shall be required as the condition of obtaining such a license." It continues, "...That motor boats shall not be required to carry licensed officers, except as required in this act."[3]

Suddenly the status of a steamboat master was reduced to the nugatory title of "motor boat operator." The station of the engineer was diminished even further. The requirement for licensed personnel in the engine-room had been eliminated, and steamboat companies could hire anyone to run the engine. Fortunately, even with the mandated change of status, the steamers were never referred to as "motor boats." They remained steamers to their last day. Through this tacit rejection of the new term, the public showed better taste than their government.

Before the Motor Boat Act, captains and engineers of passenger steamers were required to be licensed.[4] After enactment of the 1910 law, only larger passenger vessels not covered by the Motor Boat Act were required to have these licensed officers. The Steamboat Inspection Service issued licenses once a candidate had accumulated sufficient experience and had demonstrated his knowledge.

An applicant for a license as engineer had to be at least 19 years of age.[5] The inspectors were required to "...examine the applicant as to his knowledge of steam machinery, and his experience as an engineer..."[6] If the inspectors were "...satisfied that his character, habits of

Tourist came to rest on the west bank of the Damariscotta River. A water tank for the head is mounted on the starboard side. Forward of the tank is a man inspecting the damage. (Postcard from the author's collection)

life, knowledge, and experience in the duties of an engineer are all such as to authorize the belief that he is a suitable and safe person to be entrusted with the powers and duties of such a station, they shall grant him a license, authorizing him to be employed in such duties for the term of five years."[7]

One such "suitable and safe person" was Pearl E. Spear of South Bristol, Maine. Engineer Spear received his initial license as First Assistant Engineer, Inland Waters, on February 27, 1893. In May 1916, Mr. Spear assumed the duties of engineer in *Tourist*.[8] Pearl had a nephew, Everett Spear, who was born at Bristol on September 4, 1898.[9] Everett's mother, Mary (Alley) Spear,

died when he was only three years old. His father, William, died of typhoid in 1916, leaving Everett and eight brothers and sisters.[10] In 1918, Everett was living with his grandparents, Oliver and Mary Spear, and his uncle Pearl in the town of his birth.[11] Everett had an inclination toward marine engineering, and spent a good deal of time learning from his experienced uncle in the engineroom of *Tourist*.

By the time he was 19, Everett had demonstrated his engineering skills to the satisfaction of his uncle and Captain LaForest "Foss" Etheridge, owner and master of the boat. Since passage of the Motor Boat Act had negated the requirement for "licensed officers" on *Tourist*,

The starboard side of the wreck as seen from the river. (photo, MSM 74-9-195)

Everett was able to act as relief engineer for his uncle without holding a steamboat license. August 26, 1918, was one such occasion when Pearl asked Everett to cover for him because he was ill. On that fateful Monday afternoon, *Tourist* was scheduled to arrive at Cotrell's Wharf in Damariscotta at 2:15.

As *Tourist* approached the landing, Captain Etheridge rang a backing bell. "The engineer was sitting on the lower deck with his feet on the rungs of the ladder descending into the engine room when he got four bells and jingler [calling for full speed astern]. As he jumped down to respond to the bells his heel caught in the rung and he fell into the engine…"[12]

The deckhand, Collis Merrill, got a line over to Charles Etheridge and William Perkins on the dock. Despite their best efforts they could not get the eye of the line over a piling. They tried to hold it but the boat was moving too fast.[13] The tide was nearly high* and running northward with "inexorable force."[14]

Captain Etheridge rang a second astern order, again with no response.[15] The Captain shouted to Merrill to tell Spear to reverse the engine. Merrill ran to the engine-

---

*High tide was at 3:27 pm, which means that five to six knots of current was moving upstream with the boat.

room door and shouted the order to Spear.[16] Merrill testified that Spear "...had a ghastly wound* in his arm from which blood was spurting, swayed on his feet, and was pale as death."[17] His hand was on the lever, but when told to reverse, he gasped. "I can't!"[18] A journalist of the day wrote, "His hand was on the throttle but his strength had left him."[19]

The line that Merrill had managed to get ashore acted like a tether, swinging *Tourist* toward the dock. Out of control, the steamer was "...hurtled between the landing float and two motor boats parting their painters."[20] The boat hit the rocks on the east side of the river, and then the current carried it sideways into the bridge.[21]

Tourist struck the bridge on her starboard side. The stack and the pilothouse slammed into the iron framework, but did not buckle. The force of the collision careened the boat over on her port beam. The hull was carried under the bridge, heeling over on her beam end.[22] Water surged in, filling the engineroom and lower deck. The upper deck canopy collapsed over the port rail but remained attached at the stack.

---

*There are several versions of the extent of the injury to Everett Spear's arm. In some accounts the engine cuts off his arm, but this was not the case, as a post-mortem examination reported a gash on his arm. One report states that the crankshaft cut his arm when he fell into the engine. This is not likely, since the clearance between the crankshaft and the engine bed is only a fraction of an inch, which would have resulted in amputation of the arm. I suspect that Spear's arm was lacerated by the crosshead. This mechanical connection between the piston rod and the connecting rod would have been moving up and down about one stroke per second if the engine was running slowly or up to 200 times per minute if it was running at full speed. The crosshead is also at the right height to catch the arm of anyone falling toward the engine. An oil cup is attached to the crosshead. This would certainly inflict serious damage if one were to come in contact with it at any speed. The front of the engine now has a steel-plate cover to prevent accidental entanglement with the moving parts.

The distance from the steamer landing at Cotrell's Wharf to the bridge is about 170 feet. If traveling at five knots, *Tourist* would have hit the bridge about twenty seconds after Merrill first got the line over.

There were 19 passengers on board when the accident occurred.[23] "Most of the passengers were summer people returning to New York and Massachusetts. Some were hurled into the water and were picked up by rowboats from the landing float, for there were plenty at hand to cast off boats from the landing as soon as the *Tourist*'s plight was evident."[24] In his account of the accident, John Sewell states that, "Some [of the passengers] were actually spilled from the decks into the river as the ship heeled. A little boy was pulled under several times, but managed to hang on to the rail. It was reported that one young woman dove gracefully into the water and swam ashore."[25]

"Charles Etheridge, who had been on the wharf handling lines, jumped into a rowboat and picked up four passengers on his way to the wreck," reported a local paper.[26] Linwood Pierce is also credited with the rescue of several passengers.[27]

Idella Clifford Murry and her daughter Marion were aboard during the accident. Both were trapped in the cabin by the rising water. Marion grabbed her mother by the hair and pulled her out of the boat. They both made it to shore.[28] Mrs. Walter Tibbets of Rockland did not fare as well. She was thrown headlong into the engineroom directly at the open door of the firebox. She closed the door to save herself from burning, but in so doing one thumb was badly mangled. Mrs. Tibbets was carried to Dr. Parsons' office, where the thumb was amputated at the first joint. Her clothing was burned and she was badly bruised and scratched.[29] Spencer Gay was swimming from the dock at Damariscotta when the *Tourist* hit. He and his friends jumped into the water to save the passengers. They pulled out about seven people, including a baby.[30]

Other passengers on board at the time of the accident included the mother and sister of Mrs. G.I. "Sonny" Hodgdon of East Boothbay and Mrs. Bessie Thorpe of Christmas Cove.[31]

Spear made it out of the engineroom despite his wounds. Joseph Robinson of Portland heard him say, "I can't swim but I'm going to jump."[32] Mr. Robinson was the last to see the young engineer alive. It is thought that Spear feared the boiler would explode when it hit the cold water.[33] Fortunately, it did not. The *Sheepscot Echo* described the event. "When young Spear finally emerged from the engine room and jumped overboard it was noticed that one of his arms was badly injured."[34] Spear, weakened by his injury, jumped into the water. He did not make it ashore. The Bristol Board of Trade offered a reward of 25 dollars for the recovery of his body.[35] On the day following the accident, the *Bangor Daily News* ran a report of the tragedy. It verifies many of the accounts given by other witnesses and adds, "The mail was saved but the freight and personal effects of the passengers were lost."

The wreckage of *Tourist* drifted to the Newcastle side (the west bank) of the river.[36] A newspaper reported that the boat came to rest on "the shore of John M. Glidden's where she was beached without sinking."[37] The *Sheepscot Echo* added that this was 25 rods (approximately 400 feet) above the bridge.[38]

There were many fortunate passengers on *Tourist* that day – it is amazing that there were not more injuries or deaths. Two of the most fortunate people that day were Mrs. Little and her daughter, who were traveling from Squirrel Island. They had missed the boat.[39]

On September 13, the *Boothbay Register* reported that "There was a universal feeling of relief when the news came that the body of Everett Spear, the victim of the wreck of the *Tourist* last week, had been recovered last Friday [September 6] morning. It was discovered floating in the Damariscotta River nearly a mile above where the accident occurred. The son of William Spear, Everett made his home with his grandparents Oliver and Mrs. Spear and his uncle Pearl Spear. An examination of the body revealed a serious wound on his arm."[40] The official cause of death is listed as "drowning."[41] Spear was eulogized as "A cheerful, industrious boy, he had earned the good will of all who knew him." His body was interred "…at the cemetery on the 'Main.' "[42]

Initial repairs to the battered steamboat were reported in a local newspaper. "The Damariscotta River steamer *Tourist* is on the beach at Newcastle undergoing repairs. We understand that she will not go on the route again this season, but will be used in the fishing business this fall."[43] When the temporary repairs were complete, *Tourist* was towed downriver for rebuilding at the Atlantic Coast Yard (later Sample's) in Boothbay Harbor.[44] The damage to *Tourist* was estimated at $1,000, which was one quarter the value of the boat. There was no insurance.[45] After about six weeks in the yards, the renovated steamer was once again underway. The *Boothbay Register* reported, "A familiar sight not seen since last summer was the steamer *Tourist* going by on her way to Round Pond."[46] Round Pond was not a regular port of call for the steamboat, but rather the home of her owner, Captain Etheridge.

With *Tourist* out of commission, the connection between the Maine Central Railroad and down-river landings came to an abrupt halt. The *Register* described the situation: "The disabling of the *Tourist* has rendered the problem of transportation between here [South Bristol] and the railroad station a serious one. Automobiles and motor boats have been busy in conveying the traffic formerly done by the *Tourist*."[47] John Davenport writes that the 37' *Nellie G.* assumed *Tourist*'s route for the remainder of the season.[48] *Nellie G.* was usually found on the run between Boothbay Harbor and Squirrel Island.[49]

A hint of things to come was the leasing of the renovated *Tourist* on December 19, 1918 by Captain Oscar C. Randall.[50] For ten days the diminutive Damariscotta steamer operated in the waters of Casco Bay, relieving the Portland-based, Bath-Casco Bay Rapid Transit Company's steamer of the same name while she underwent repairs.*

The year 1919 brought changes in boat service to the Damariscotta River. In March, Captain Mark Thompson began daily service to all of the former Damariscotta Steamboat Company's landings with his motor boat *Pilgrim*.[51] Late in the spring of 1919 the renovated *Tourist* re-entered the steamboat trade at South Bristol, making two trips per day with Captain Thompson at the helm.[52]

June 1919 was a bad month for *Tourist*. Prior to the summer season, she had her boiler retubed and engine overhauled.[53] By June 27, she was out of commission with boiler and machinery problems that had to be repaired at Boothbay Harbor.[54] In less than a month, the boiler tubes were failing once again.[55] One week later, four more tubes let go.[56] As if to add insult to injury, the mail carrier, Lewis Tarr, announced that he would carry passengers and the mail between South Bristol and

Damariscotta in his seven-passenger automobile. He added, "Others have cars which are to be available for trips anywhere and everywhere."[57]

By mid-August, Captain Etheridge had reached a point of frustration that called for desperate action. He removed the ailing *Tourist* from service and moored her at Round Pond.[58] One week later he purchased a motor boat named *Kraken* from the estate of Judge Thompson of Greenfield, Massachusetts, and continued mail and passenger service with it for the remainder of the season.[59] In 1920 Captain Mark Thompson had "a new and powerful" Palmer engine installed in *Pilgrim*[60] and Randall Harrington was named as captain of Foss Etheridge's former boat *Kraken*, which he renamed *Celia E.*[61] In June of 1920 the *Lincoln County News* published an ominous notice. "There will be a special meeting of the stockholders of the Damariscotta Steamboat Company [sic]* at the Newcastle National Bank, Damariscotta, Maine, on Thursday, July 1, 1920 at 10 o'clock a.m., to act on the following business. To fill three vacancies on the Board of Directors. To see if the stockholders will vote to dissolve the corporation, Damariscotta Steamboat Company, and authorize the Board of Directors to take such action to close the business and affairs of the company as may be required."[62]

It appears that the board voted to dissolve the steamboat company. *Tourist* did not operate on the river in 1920, although LaForest Etheridge was still listed owner.[63] The *Maine Register*, which had properly noted the name change to Damariscotta Steamboat Line in 1918,[64] showed another name change to Damariscotta

_____

*The confusion created by two steamboats of the same name in the same waters would further be compounded when the Damariscotta's *Tourist* (after a name change to *Sabino*) was sold for regular service in Casco Bay. Passengers today still confuse the 1913-built *Tourist* with the earlier 1908 boat on which they are riding. Fortunately, no one today is old enough to remember the Tourist Steamboat Line of Casco Bay and their namesake steamer from 1871.

_____

*Even though LaForest Etheridge changed the name of the company to the Damariscotta Steamboat Line when he bought it in 1917, local usage still reflected the original designation.

River Line in the 1919-20 edition.[65] This change reflects the retirement of *Tourist* and her replacement with a gasoline-powered boat. LaForest Etheridge and Mark Thompson continued to operate mail and passenger service on the Damariscotta River; however, it was now accomplished by gasoline boat and automobile.[66] In fact, contracts for mail service to Christmas Cove[67] and Round Pond were awarded to the two former river captains in 1921. The same year, Mark Thompson is listed as the owner of the Damariscotta River Line.[68]

In July 1921 an attempt to revive steamboat service was announced in the local newspaper. The Kennebec Navigation Company attempted service between Bath and Christmas Cove. "All here [South Bristol] hope it will be a success and look for the old steamboat days to return."[69] Yet in September the *Lincoln County News* lamented the passing of steamboat service with the following epitaph: "The Kennebec Navigation Company deserves the thanks of all for their effort to give us a steamboat connection. The auto travel has injured this line of business we fear beyond repair."[70]

With this stark statement, steamboat transportation on the Damariscotta River drew to an unceremonious close.

On October 8, 1921, Captain Etheridge sold *Tourist*, the last steamer of the original Damariscotta Steamboat Company, to the Popham Beach Steamboat Company on the neighboring Kennebec River.[71]

The process of salvaging *Tourist* involved removal of the canopy and stabilizing the hull with floats attached to each side. The water was then pumped out and the boat towed to Boothbay Harbor for repairs. (Harold Castner collection, courtesy of Ruth Woods)

In the new design, *Sabino* had two bulkheads separating the engineroom from fresh, outside air. The sliding doors installed during this rebuild have been repaired through the years but still look the same today. (W.H. Ballard Collection, courtesy of Diane Ballard Michael)

CHAPTER 5

A BOAT TO THE BEACH

STEAMBOATING ARRIVED EARLY on the Kennebec River. As the War of 1812 raged to the south, Jonathan Morgan was busy building a steamboat at Alna, Maine. With more ambition than knowledge, the enterprising Mr. Morgan entered the new world of steam engineering. Less prepared than most other steamboat experimenters, Morgan and his associates had neither drawings nor descriptions from which to design their steamboat – in fact, none of them had ever seen a steam engine. It is not surprising that their first engine did not work and "was flung away."[1]

In 1815, Morgan built another engine, and although this one worked it was too small for practical use in his 16-ton boat. The following year he enlarged his engine, and finally was able to leave the dock at the conservative speed of four miles per hour. Later that year Morgan went to Brunswick and built a boat of about 30 tons in which he installed a new engine. A noteworthy point of this vessel's construction was its boiler: It was made of wood.* More specifically, it was "built of pine plank, and about the size of a common molasses hogshead." The boat also featured a screw propeller, a propulsion system well ahead of its time.[2] This pioneering effort led a

parade of steamboats and steamboat companies, each of which contributed to the evolution of commercial navigation in the region.

The size and status of Kennebec River vessels matched the diversity of the communities they served. There were large, deep-draft steamers such as the 317-foot *Ransom B. Fuller* that provided the most modern conveniences for passengers traveling between Bath and Boston.[3] At the other end of the scale were diminutive local boats such as the 35-foot *Lizzie M. Snow*. These small boats shuttled between major steamer docks and less prominent landings along the river.[4] This network of steamboats provided a variety of services from the Kennebec's head of navigation to its mouth at Popham Beach.

---

*This unlikely material has been well-documented in American boiler construction since 1800. Oliver Evans built a boiler of five-inch pine planks braced with ten-inch square oak beams and stayed with one-and-a-quarter-inch rods. Details of construction and drawings can be found in Louis C. Hunter, *A History of Industrial Power in the United States, 1780-1930*, Vol. 2 (Charlottesville, Virginia: University of Virginia, 1985), 306-07.

Captain James E. Perkins, the man who gave *Sabino* her name, was general manager of the Popham Beach Steamboat Company until 1927 when the last boat, *Sabino*, was sold. (Captain James E. Perkins Collection, courtesy of Jane W. Stevens)

A new name and a new look came in 1922 as *Sabino* (ex-*Tourist*) began service between Bath and Popham Beach. (W.H. Ballard Collection, courtesy of Diane Ballard Michael)

The crew of *Percy V.* (left to right): Sylvanus Wallace, Captain James E. Perkins, Fred Hodgkins, and Frank Stevens. Fred and Jim began steamboating together at the age of fifteen as two of the original crew of *Percy V.* Captain Jim continued with the company until *Sabino* was the only boat left on the line. (Captain James E. Perkins Collection, courtesy of Jane W. Stevens)

"Three miles of the most perfect beach to be found anywhere in the world…" is Jane Stevens' description of her favorite spot on earth.[5] This enthusiastic opinion of Popham Beach is shared by many, and has been for several generations. One steamboat company touted Popham as "…the grandest beach in all New England."[6] The beach is named in honor of George Popham, who first settled the shores of the Kennebec some 13 years before the Pilgrims landed at Plymouth. Prior to the arrival of European settlers, Native Americans of the Abenaki tribe sought fish and shellfish in the area.

In the years following the Civil War, steamboat enterprises throughout New England boomed. At first, service to Popham Beach was sporadic, with irregular visits by Captain McLellan in his little steamer *Anemone.*

Scheduled service to the popular summer spot arrived with *Creedmore* in 1878.[7] Over the next 25 years, a dozen steamers brought vacationers to the sands of Popham Beach at various times.

The citizens at Popham were enthusiastic supporters of the steamers, and the beach soon became a popular respite from city temperatures during hot New England summers. Sensing that Popham Beach had the potential to rival Mount Desert as a summer resort, several residents formed an improvement association to promote their community. One of their paramount goals was to establish frequent, regular steamboat service between Popham and Bath.

On June 12, 1883, *Percy V.* was launched from the yards of C.B. Harrington at Bath. The 65' steamer was

Sabino hauled out at Goudy & Stevens yard, East Boothbay, in 1925. The reason for the haulout was to repair the damage done when they "knocked the stern post out of her" during a race with the tug *Seguin*. (Captain James E. Perkins Collection, courtesy of Jane W. Stevens)

built for the Popham Beach Summer Resort Association* and named for Percy O. Vickery of Augusta, who had been an early developer of Popham as a summer resort. *Percy V.* was under the command of Captain George W. Stacey, with 16-year-old James E. Perkins as mate and Frank Lockery as engineer.[8]

Percy V. soon became famous for her transit time–not the sort of fame to which a captain aspires. She was slow–intolerably slow. One comparison declared that "…she was a poor bet in a race with a snow plow."[9] As if to add insult to injury, *Percy V.* was known to take a

schooner in tow for the passage upriver to Bath during regularly scheduled passenger trips.[10] On these occasions, the endurance and indulgence of the passengers were pushed to the limit. When speaking of this practice, Captain P.O. Haley of Parker Head quipped, "It paid for the coal."[11]

Jim Perkins ascended to the helm of *Percy V.* in 1888 and remained her master until October 1897 when the vessel was sold to Portland parties.[12] Soon after the sale, the Eastern Steamboat Company put *Winter Harbor* on the run to Popham Beach. Captain Perkins became master, Frank A. Oliver was engineer, and Augustus Hodkins was mate.[13]

Winter Harbor was the first boat to attempt a 12-month schedule. Landings were advertised for Phippsburg, Hinckley's Landing (West Georgetown), Parker Head, Cox's Head, Bay Point, and Popham Beach.

---

*There are a number of variations on the name of this association. Baker gives it as the Popham Beach Hotel & Real Estate Company. Cram lists it as the Fort Popham Summer Resident Association while newspaper notes give it as the Fort Popham Summer Resort Association.

Year-round service between Bath and Popham Beach was the goal of Captain Perkins and the Popham Beach Steamboat Company. *Sabino* was surrounded by ice when the photograph was taken. Note the wheel chair on the upper deck. (Courtesy of Maine Maritime Museum, Bath, Maine)

Sabino underway at full speed of about eight knots on the waters of the Kennebec River. (Captain James E. Perkins Collection, courtesy of Jane W. Stevens)

Sabino had a slim appearance when she ran on the Kennebec River. Two men work on the sternpost repair while a spectator, sporting knickers, looks on. (Captain James E. Perkins Collection, courtesy of Jane W. Stevens)

The severity of the winter of 1897-98 brought service to an abrupt halt when *Winter Harbor* lost her propeller in an ice jam.[14] Steamboat service resumed with the arrival of spring.

In July 1898, *Winter Harbor* went to Boothbay Harbor for the summer season. The 66' steamer *Gardiner* was leased from the Augusta-Gardiner Steamboat Company to cover the run to Popham. Again, Captain Perkins was in the pilothouse with the crew from *Winter Harbor* augmented by Hiram Stevens, purser, and Albert Spinney, fireman.

Captain Perkins was quite a sportsman and, like many from that era and locale, a frugal Yankee. In keeping with both of these qualities, the good captain kept a shotgun in the pilothouse. If a goose flew too close to the steamer he would bag the fowl and make a small deviation from his course to retrieve his quarry.[15] What is not reported is the reaction of the engineer to the sudden blast of a shotgun from the boat. When standing next to a boiler with 150 pounds per square inch on the gauge, any sudden noise can punctuate the day with momentary terror.

On March 12, 1901, the Eastern Steamship Company was formed through the absorption of the Kennebec Steamboat Company and its subsidiary, the Eastern Steamboat Company. As a stabilizing gesture, the new company retained James D. Drake as president. Drake had presided over the Eastern Steamboat Company since 1896.[16]

Winter Harbor was owned by the new company and continued to operate on the Bath-to-Boothbay Harbor run. Eastern's *Damarin* assumed the Bath-to-Popham Beach route. This venerable steamer started life as *Samoset*, but was renamed after her 1894 hull rebuild. The additional 18" of draft and 4' of length supported an entirely new superstructure. The renovated *Damarin* provided service to the beach from 1899 through 1903.[17]

As the Eastern Steamship Company reorganized its schedule and re-distributed its vessels, some routes were abandoned. Service between Bath and Popham Beach ended in 1903.[18] The abrupt halt in steamboat service compelled the citizens at the beach to take action. In November 1903, the Popham Beach Steamboat Company was founded. *Winter Harbor* was purchased from the Eastern Steamship Company and year-round service began under the new banner.[19]

Finding that they needed a bigger boat, the Popham Beach Steamboat Company purchased the 73' *Eldorado* from the Casco Bay Steamboat Company in 1904. This was the largest of the Popham steamers and Captain Perkins' favorite during his many years on the river. *Eldorado*'s end came when she burned to the waterline at her Popham pier in December 1908.[20] On January 11, 1909, the Popham Beach Steamboat Company was back in operation with the chartered steamer *Jule*. In May, the Kelley, Spear Company launched the new steamer *Virginia*. *Virginia*'s designers were Ernest F. Kelley and J. Arthur Stevens.* She was registered as 66.3' long, 18.5' beam and 6.3' depth with a gross tonnage of 71, and Captain Perkins was her master for all 12 years of her service on the Kennebec.[21]

In September 1921, *Virginia* was sold to the Augusta, Gardiner & Boothbay Steamboat Company. In order to maintain service to Bath, the Popham Beach Steamboat Company purchased *Tourist* from LaForest Etheridge on October 8, 1921,[22] for the sum of $2,000.[23]

The first thing Captain Perkins did with the new boat was change the name. He chose to call her *Sabino* after Sabino Hill, his favorite spot at Popham.[24] This hill rises 115 feet above Atkins Bay on the west shore of the Kennebec River. From its peak, one can survey the entire

---

*J. Arthur Stevens' daughter Sibyl was Captain Jim Perkins' wife.

village of Popham Beach or, looking north, see halfway to Bath. To the east is Cape Newagen, the geographical boundary between Sheepscot Bay and Booth Bay. The most imposing view is to the south, where ships a dozen miles distant can be observed with curious speculation as to their origin and destination. The United States government recognized the strategic importance of the Sabino Hill vantage point. Between 1908 and 1912, they built Fort Baldwin at the top of the hill, installing a lookout tower and three gun emplacements to guard the entrance to the Kennebec River.

The origin of the name "Sabino" is Native American. At the time George Popham was establishing a settlement at the foot of Sabino Hill, he encountered a local sagamore of the Abenaki tribe.[25] As Popham wrote of him, "his name that Came unto us ys Sabenoa. he macks hemselffe unto us to be Lord of the ryver of Sagadahoc." The quote in quaint English is from George Popham's, *The Relation of a Voyage to Sagadahoc 1607-1608.* The date of the entry is September 26, 1607.[26]

The name "Sabino," a corruption of Sabenoa, applied to both the chief and his village in the seventeenth century.[27] Today it names the hill marking the summer encampment of the Abenaki.

When the Popham Beach Steamboat Company took title to *Sabino*, she was tired. A 1921 financial statement from the company details the bad news: "Paid alteration and repairs, including railway bill, retubing boiler, repairs to engine and hull and all other work, until boat was ready to go on route...$4,736,86."[28] The repairs were more than twice the purchase price of the boat. The refit was accomplished at Bath Iron Works.[29]

To go with her new name, *Sabino* got a new look. The pilothouse was raised about two feet, which made its deck the same height as the upper deck of the boat. An exterior bulkhead with seven windows on each side was constructed at the rail, extending from a point under the pilothouse door to the forward end of the lady's cabin. This resulted in enclosing the passageway alongside the engineroom, leaving the existing engineroom bulkhead intact. The head, which had been added midway through her Damariscotta years, was moved forward. This encroached on the lady's cabin but provided a passageway around the stern. A stairway was constructed from the aftermost point of the main deck to the upper deck. A canopy over the upper deck extended from the rear of the pilothouse to the stern. *Sabino* is thought by many to have achieved her most attractive configuration during this period.

When *Sabino* began her first season on the Kennebec in 1922, the auto industry added more than two and a half million cars to America's roadways.[30] It was only a matter of time before the popularity of the automobile would once again diminish the appeal of steamboat transportation–not only among the passengers but among the steamboat men. The public's waning fondness for steamboat travel was reflected in the disappointment of some of the steamboat crews. Captain Perkins, with nearly 40 years on Popham Beach steamers, was now master of a vessel that was 20' shorter than his first command. One morning in 1927, the Captain began his usual walk down to the dock to take *Sabino* on the upriver trip to Bath. The tide was low. As he reached a point halfway down the dock, the veteran mariner came to a stop. He paused for a moment, then slowly turned around and returned home. Placing his hat on its familiar hook he retired from steamboating with the resolute quotation, "When they're so small you can't see the stack above the wharf, that's the end of steamboating."[31]

On July 23, 1927, *Sabino* was sold to Harry P. Williams of Portland[32] and the books of the Popham Beach Steamboat Company were closed.

This 1935 photograph shows *Sabino* at the beginning of her Casco Bay Lines career. Note the short stack, open foredeck on both levels, and the lifeboat on the canopy. (Courtesy of the Steamship Historical Society Collection, Providence, Rhode Island)

CHAPTER 6

THE CASCO BAY YEARS

AS THE NUMBER OF AUTOMOBILES multiplied, the popularity of steamboat travel continued to decline. The independence of leaving at any time and driving wherever one wanted could not be matched by the steamboat companies.

In another devastating blow, the streetcar companies had developed a network of interconnecting lines by the 1920s. Passengers could travel from points as distant as New York City to the resort areas of Portland, Maine, if they chose, entirely by trolley car.

Open trolleys lined with as many as 15 benches were popular on the hot days of the New England summer. By riding the open cars, a traveler could enjoy the cooling coastal breeze without the frequently nauseating effect of boat travel. The trolleys featured more frequent departures from a variety of convenient locations. Their ability to travel at 25 miles per hour made the five- or six-knot speed of a steamboat seem archaic.

Despite the increased miles of roadway and trolley track, there was one thing the land-based conveyances could not accomplish. They could not provide trans-portation between the mainland and the hundreds of islands that dotted the coast of Maine.

One area of the rock-bound coast with an abundance of islands is Casco Bay. Stretching nearly 18 miles northeast of Maine's largest city, Portland, the bay is dotted with islands that range in size from little more than a rock to those "...which are three or four miles in length, having well laid out roads, making driving a pleasure, and which are good size settlements with their own churches, stores and other accessories of a town."[1]

The romantic notion of the 365 "Calendar Islands" of Casco Bay seems to have originated in a British report of 1691 which reads, in part, "...There be a coved bay, so bay of great and small islands, truly as many as the days in a yr."[2] According to the U.S. Coast Pilot, there are 136 islands of inhabitable size.[3]

Seasonal travelers have visited the Casco Bay area for centuries. Lief Ericson is reported to have landed on the islands as early as 1000 AD. The French, in the 1500s, were the first Europeans to attempt permanent settlements. By 1652, this area, along with the rest of Maine, became part of the Massachusetts Bay Colony and remained a portion of Massachusetts until 1820, when Maine joined the union as a separate state.[4]

The first steamboat service to the islands of Casco Bay is credited to Captain Seward Porter and his steamer *Kennebec* in 1822. Other ventures were attempted from time to time in the first half of the nineteenth century, with regular service being established in 1850 by Captain Horatio G. Cook, Jr. with the steamers *Antelope* and successor vessels.

In the century that followed, the evolution of steamboat service in Casco Bay produced as many stories as there are islands. No attempt will be made here to document the genealogy of the steamboat lines of Casco Bay.* What will be attempted is a thorough documentation of *Sabino*'s years on this lovely stretch of the Maine coast.

*Captain William J. Frappier has ably accomplished the task of documenting the history of steamboats on Casco Bay in his book, *Steamboat Yesterdays on Casco Bay*.

Harry P. Williams found *Sabino* to roll quite a bit in the open waters of Casco Bay. During the winter of 1927-28 he added sponsons to give her more beam and thus more stability. Passengers could now walk from stem to stern on the main deck without passing through the main cabin. (Courtesy of Portland Newspapers)

Harry P. Williams and his younger brother Fred. L. immigrated to Portland from West Bath, Maine, in 1908. Together they established a machine-shop business under the name of the Williams Brothers Company at 495 Fore Street. In 1910 they moved their business onto Custom House Wharf, where it remained in the family until 1953.[5]

It appears that Harry and Fred did not always get along. In 1914 Harry left the machine-shop business and went out on his own in the boat repair and machinist trade. By 1917, Harry had mended fences and the two brothers began a new venture as steamboat operators. In their 1917 report to the Public Utilities Commission, the Cape Shore Ferry Company reported that, "Williams Bros., Custom House Wharf, leased the Cape Shore Ferry Company for the season of 1917 and commenced running the boats July 4, 1917 until sometime in September."[6] The following year, Harry and Fred successfully bid on a surplus navy steam launch at a government sale. This 13-year veteran was rebuilt, enlarged, and launched as *Admiral* in recognition of her naval origin.

During the rebuild, the Williams Brothers increased the beam of the boat by adding sponsons. Sponsons are attachments to a boat that make the hull wider. They are watertight and have the appearance of a pontoon, sliced longitudinally, affixed to the hull. They have the effect of making the boat more stable while increasing the deck area above.

Admiral seems to have been one of the navy's standard 40' steam cutters of the 1898 design. These utilitarian craft had a length between perpendiculars equal to *Admiral*'s registered length of 38'.[7] Even with the 6' extension to her stern made by the Williams Brothers, the length between perpendiculars would have remained the same. A navy-built compound engine with the designation of E-2 powered the 40' steam cut-

ters. The 5 & 10.5 x 8 engine developed 48.87 horsepower at 350 rpm with a boiler pressure of 160 psi. The boiler was a type G-1 Ward water tube.[8]

Harry Williams ran the Cape Shore Ferry Company from 1917 through 1921 from Cape Elizabeth. In 1921, he moved the operation to Portland.[9] This same year, Oscar Randall offered his steamers *Gurnet* and *Tourist** for sale. Harry wanted to buy them and the rights to their landings in order to expand the steamboat business; Fred did not. The brothers could not come to an agreement, and Oscar Randall's boats and business were purchased by Casco Bay Lines.[10]

By 1924, the business for *Admiral* had reached an all-time low. Both brothers recognized the gravity of the situation, but could not agree on a solution. Again the brothers parted ways, with Harry taking control of *Admiral* and Fred assuming control of the machine-shop business.[11] Harry discontinued the Cape Cottage-Cushing-Peaks Island route, much to the consternation of Cushing Islanders. He took over the night runs to Little Diamond, Peaks, Great Diamond, and Long Island which had been served by the Randall steamers. Then he purchased the little steamer *Lottie and May* to serve as an excursion vessel and backup boat for the aging *Admiral. Lottie and May* covered the scheduled service while *Admiral* underwent an unprecedented metamorphosis. Cooperating as brothers –a rare event indeed– Harry and Fred removed *Admiral*'s tired steam plant and installed a three-cylinder Bessemer diesel. This was the first marine diesel on the Portland waterfront. Despite her new plant, she was referred to as the "steamer" *Admiral.*

The modest boat line prospered during the last half of

---

*This is the 1913 *Tourist*, not to be confused with *Sabino* under her former name.

the 1920s. Service was extended to a year-round venture, and Harry Williams added a second captain to the operation. Captain George "Cliff" Randall, a veteran of several day steamers, signed on as the business continued to grow. By 1927, patronage had reached a point where it became obvious that the company needed another boat. On September 15, 1927, the steamer *Sabino* was added to the Williams' fleet list.[12]

Sabino immediately took over the run to the islands, replacing *Admiral*.[13] The *Portland Press Herald* reported that, "She is considered to be a great improvement over *Admiral* inasmuch as there is a separate saloon for ladies."[14] The arrival of the new boat was reflected in a new name for the company. "Steamers *Admiral* and *Sabino*" became the banner for the company based on the Portland pier. Captain Williams commanded *Sabino* on her run between Portland and Peaks Island, while Captain Randall ran *Admiral* directly from Portland to Cushing Island.

Sabino had a longstanding reputation as a top-heavy boat, dating from her years on the Damariscotta River. The caption for a photo taken aboard her before 1913 notes that, "For a wonder, she wasn't rolling much; usually the passengers looked a little more apprehensive."[15] If a boat rolls in a river, as *Sabino* notoriously did, it can be expected that a ride on the far-less-sheltered waters of Casco Bay could be a real adventure. Finding that this was the case, Captain Williams added sponsons to *Sabino* during her first winter layup in 1927-28. He extended the main deck over the sponsons to a solid bulwark, making a walkway around the engineroom. The main cabin and upper deck were left intact, giving *Sabino* the somewhat ungainly appearance of a boat sitting on a bigger boat.

Captain Williams again changed the name of his steamboat line. Perhaps a purist had once too often called Harry's attention to the fact that he was calling a diesel boat a steamer. Whatever the reason, "Steamers *Admiral* and *Sabino*" became the "Island Evening Line" in the summer of 1933. Under the new company name, *Sabino* made 17 trips per day between Portland and Peaks Island.[16]

Harry Williams began yet another enterprise on the Portland Pier. In 1933 he opened a small pierside restaurant under the name of the "Anchor Lunch." He hoped to serve the passengers of the Evening Line as well as those of the double-ended ferry to Peaks Island, *Swampscott*. The restaurant must have become a going concern requiring more attention from its owner. The 1935 edition of the *Casco Bay Directory* lists Captain Cliff Randall as the master of *Sabino*.[17]

On July 23, 1935, Harry P. Williams sold *Sabino* to the Casco Bay Lines.[18] Captain Williams' steamboat line had dwindled once again to a single boat, *Admiral*. The operation of the solitary vessel was known as the Cushing Island Boat Company. This service continued until 1943.[19]

In tracing the family tree of Casco Bay Lines, one finds a lineage dating from the earliest steamboat entrepreneurs.* The first 80 years of commercial service on the bay saw many companies founder and disappear. Some lost their individual identities through mergers and survived only in memory through the vessels they had built.

The 1907 consolidation of the Casco Bay Steamboat Company (second of that name) and the Harpswell Steamboat Company resulted in the Casco Bay & Harpswell Lines.[20] This company was the amalgamation of many of the early defunct carriers. The union of these

---

*In a promotional publication entitled *The Casco Bay Islands*, the Casco Bay Lines claims, "During the past 148 years Casco Bay Line has carried over 74 million passengers on a year-round basis!" With a publication date of around 1969, this would seem to claim a lineage to the first steamer on the bay around 1822.

two lines resulted in eight steamers to serve the bay plus a South Portland ferry steamer and a steam lighter for freight, dock repairs, and other miscellaneous duties. Casco Bay & Harpswell Lines provided service for a dozen years, ceasing operations on September 30, 1919.[21]

From the ashes of Casco Bay & Harpswell Lines emerged the Casco Bay Lines. This company survives today, providing ferry services to the islands off Portland. The boats departing from the Custom House Wharf may lack the warmth and charm of the steamers, but the service endures.

At some point between the time when *Sabino* received her sponsons in 1927-28 and the union with the Casco Bay Lines, the veteran steamboat underwent another metamorphosis to equip her better for the waters off Portland. The walkway over the sponsons was enclosed and benches were installed facing inboard. The engine-room bulkhead was replaced with a banister-type railing that provided a clear view of the engine and boiler from the comfort of the benches. Those who dared could offer their suggestions to the engineer from the barroom-height railing overlooking the machinery. Despite the

Sabino in her wartime gray paint scheme. In addition to a change in color, many structural changes had been completed by World War II. A stairway had been constructed forward of the lengthened stack, an awning extends forward of the pilothouse, the maindeck was enclosed to house a lifejacket locker and provide protection for freight, and a "cattle fence" replaced the rope netting. (Postcard from the author's collection)

Sabino at Portland in 1947. At the end of the war, *Sabino* returned to her original white paint scheme. Note the addition of a single ventilator on the starboard side of the stack. Both *Sabino* and *Tourist* (1913) have steam up. *Maquoit* and *Aucosisco* lay alongside the pier with another steamer, probably *Emita*, last in the line. (Photo by William A. Burke, courtesy of Richard Burke)

kibitzers, the engineers must have felt as if they had been released from a closet when the athwartship dimension between the engineroom bulkheads went from 9' to 21'.

The Casco Bay Lines* registered *Sabino* on June 27, 1935, and named Cliff Randall as her master.[22] When Captain Randall moved *Sabino* around from Portland

*The story of *Sabino* in the service of Casco Bay Lines is from Jim Millinger's article "The Steamer *Sabino* on Casco Bay, 1927-1961" as published in The *Log of Mystic Seaport*, Autumn 1995. Mr. Millinger's thorough research makes any attempt by me to cover the material an exercise in redundancy. I appreciate his scholarly work and reproduce it here virtually verbatim. His endnotes are included.

Pier to Custom House Wharf, her arrival brought the number of vessels in the Casco Bay Lines fleet to six. These vessels would remain the core of Casco Bay Lines service on the bay for the next 15 years. These vessels were all constructed of wood, and all had originally been propelled by steam. Like Harry Williams' *Admiral*, two of them had been converted to diesel propulsion in the mid-1920s.

For the busy summer season, the queen of the fleet, the *Aucosisco*, the *Maquoit*, and the much smaller *Sabino* were brought out of winter layup to supplement the three workhorse vessels of the year-round fleet, the diesels *Emita* and *Gurnet* and the steam-powered *Tourist*. The *Emita* and the *Gurnet* were used year-round because their diesel engines made them the most inexpensive to operate. If a third winter boat were needed, *Tourist* was the choice rather than *Sabino* because she had more enclosed passenger space and was a better sea

boat. Although older than *Tourist* and *Gurnet*, *Sabino* was considered the "junior" of the three smaller vessels. She was newer to the fleet, she carried fewer passengers, and, despite her sponsors, she was the least comfortable in any kind of sea.

The Casco Bay Lines made significant capital improvements to *Sabino*. First, probably in the winter of 1936-37, the company completed the transformation of her superstructure by moving the rail and canopy out to the edge of the upper deck.[23] Then it turned its attention to her propulsion. In order to improve the draft in her boiler, a short stack of narrower diameter was placed on top of her smokestack. Pictures indicate this occurred no earlier than the winter of 1937-38.

In the winter of 1940-41 the company replaced her old boiler with an Almy water-tube boiler. To increase the draft of her new boiler, *Sabino*'s stack was further lengthened with a 6' extension at this time.[†]

[†]There are differing versions of when *Sabino* received her new boiler and stack. The *Portland Sunday Telegraph Sun* wrote on 11 June 1967 that the "Almy water-tube boiler was new in 1947." This must be in error, for the first visual evidence of the 6' stack extension, which most agree came with the new boiler, is in a picture of *Sabino* in her wartime coat of gray paint. The Casco Bay Lines vessels were repainted white before June 1946. Therefore, the new stack must have been added sometime before June 1946.

In 1968, David Crockett, in "A Short History of the Steamer *Sabino*," published in the Spring 1968 issue of *Steamboat Bill*, placed the first stack change before the boiler replacement: "Also, an extension was added to her stack, but of smaller diameter than the existing pipe....During World War II, she received the present Almy water-tube boiler." He did not comment on the 6' extension.

In 1974, David Dodge et al., in *Steamer Sabino*, commented: "Sometime during the Second World War *Sabino* received her present Almy Water-tube boiler, replacing her original fire-tube type. Her stack was also lengthened to improve draft."

In 1986 or after, Robert W. Morse wrote in his report, "The

Restoration/Reconstruction of *Sabino* 1974-86": "*Sabino* had her smoke stack lengthened when she received a new water-tube boiler which replaced her old fire-tube one in 1941." I assume that he is referring to the 6' extension rather than the new short stack, but his next sentence reads: "A pipe and canvas awning has been added over the fore passenger deck." This was added at the time of the addition of the new short stack, which pictorial evidence places as early as summer 1938.

The first pictorial evidence of her 6' stack extension is in a wartime photograph taken no later than June 1946. If she got one of these new stacks at the same time as her boiler replacement, it was probably the second. The two "early" sources (1968 and 1974) put the boiler replacement during World War II. Two later sources (1986, and Captain John Hunter, who commanded *Sabino* at Mystic Seaport) put it in 1941. If they are reporting seeing the new boiler and lengthened stack during her summer 1941 season, then the conversion would have been made in the winter of 1940-41, and would have been before, not "during" World War II. (The builder's plate on the boiler bears the construction date of 1940, which further supports Jim Millinger's belief that the work was done in the winter of 1940-41. GK III).

Despite these improvements *Sabino*'s role in the bay changed very little. She was still used as the summer night boat to Peaks Island, which meant that she normally ran only in the upper bay, only in the summertime, and only in the late afternoon and at night.[24] Although she was designated as the "back-up" vessel during the daytime (and her coal fire was kept banked in readiness), she didn't come alive until her engineer and master came on board in the mid-afternoon. She then made six scheduled trips to the islands. On the 4:10 p.m.–the banker's special–Cliff Randall took her to the two Diamond Islands, the three landings at Peaks Island, and then across the exposed Hussey Sound to Ponce Landing on Long Island. He then took her to Forest City Landing at Peaks Island on the remaining five trips (6:15, 7:15, 8:15, 9:15, and 11:15 p.m.) with an additional stop at Trefeathen Landing on Peaks Island on the 9:15 p.m.[25]

With the outbreak of World War II, the U.S. Navy came to Casco Bay because of its natural protection and the depth of its available anchorage space. The U.S. Army Coast Artillery came as well to provide the fleet with the protection of its guns. Each had its own transportation system, in part using former civilian vessels. The U.S. Navy took *Aucosisco* from the Casco Bay Lines, the U.S. Army took *Admiral* from Harry Williams, and both services chartered *Maquoit* with a Casco Bay Lines crew.[26]

For her part, *Sabino* was painted gray and a final superstructure change was made to increase her versatility. The Casco Bay Lines turned her canopy into a third, hurricane deck by building a set of steps between the pilothouse and stack from the upper deck to the canopy level and fashioning a pipe handrail for those climbing the steps and as a support and enclosure for passengers in the loading area on the hurricane deck. This enabled *Sabino* to land at very high piers and approach others at very low tide.[27] The company also enclosed *Sabino*'s bow between the upper and lower decks. This might have been done prior to the winter of 1942-43, when there is some evidence she was used in the winter season for the only time in her service as a Casco Bay Lines vessel.[28]

Sabino got some wartime publicity when the local newspapers reported that the Zukunft sisters of Peaks Island were working on her as pursers. During and just after the war, Ellen, Marie, Catherine, and Joan Zukunft worked aboard *Sabino* as they made their way through college and in and out of military service. This was a "first" in the Casco Bay Lines fleet, and the newspapers made much of their contribution to the war effort and their working in what had been an all-male occupation.

Their opportunity may have been a result of a *Sabino* peculiarity and a legacy from Harry Williams. *Sabino* steamed with a crew of four: a licensed master, a licensed engineer, a purser, and a deckhand. She did not carry a mate. From the time the vessel prepared to back away from Custom House Wharf the captain was fully occupied with his duties in the pilothouse, and the engineer remained in the boiler and engine space, ready to respond to the captain's bell signals at any time. The purser took tickets at the gangway, and the deckhand tended the spring line that held the vessel to the wharf. All of the Casco Bay Lines vessels except *Sabino* used a spring line with a big eye-splice in one end which the mate heaved over the head of a piling when the vessel came alongside a wharf. He then shouted instructions down to the deckhand, who tended the length of the line on a set of bitts on the lower deck while the captain gave bell signals to the engineer to move the vessel ahead or astern in order to position the gangway at the appropriate spot on the wharf. *Sabino* had a hook attached to the end of her spring line, and the process of hooking and tending the line was done from the lower deck by one man–the deckhand or "hookman." Once *Sabino* was in position, the purser went to the lower deck to heave the gangplank across to the wharf with the deckhand. Or, if the upper-deck gangplank were to be used, the deckhand scampered up the ladder to assist. The purser never had to heave the line. Marie Zukunft Graves believes that this is why women could be pursers, but not mates. If so, it was a legacy from Harry Williams's ownership, for *Admiral* was the only other vessel in the bay that had a hook.[29]

After World War II, the Office of Marine Inspection of the U.S. Coast Guard began to enforce a series of regulations meant to retire unsafe vessels. The 45-year-old *Maquoit* was condemned in 1949. The 55-year-old *Aucosisco* made her last trip down the bay on November 4, 1952, and a few months later the 72-year-old *Emita* made her last trip on Valentine's Day 1953. Two years later the 42-year-old *Tourist* was deactivated.[30]

As these vessels left service, a new Casco Bay Lines management continued to implement the transition to diesel power that had begun in the mid-1920s. The company bought two wooden diesel-powered vessels to serve Peaks Island–the 54' *Narmada* as a car ferry, and the 50.5' *Sunshine* as a passenger vessel. And they had two steel diesel-powered vessels, *Aucosisco II* and *Emita II*, built at the Blount shipyard of Rhode Island for service down the bay. Only two of the old fleet were left: the diesel-powered *Gurnet*, built in 1914, and the steamer *Sabino*.

In hopes of providing more timely and dependable passenger service, the new management turned *Gurnet* into a freight boat. This allowed the passenger boats to make quick stops for passengers and the mail without long delays while freight was off-loaded at the island landings. The day-trippers enjoyed the work-boat atmosphere as the passenger boats loaded and unloaded freight, but the "regulars," who might be attempting to keep appointments or meet buses or planes in Portland, did not appreciate the long delays.

In this transition *Sabino* was replaced in her role as night boat to Peaks Island by *Sunshine*. When Cliff Randall, her skipper on this route for more than 29 years, shifted his long watch from the pilothouse of the steamer to the pilothouse of the diesel-powered *Sunshine*, *Sabino* was sent to the head of the dock and relegated to back-up vessel.[31] For three summers she remained at the head of the dock, getting occasional use when one of the other vessels in the fleet broke down or when there was a special charter. But as a run-down holdover from an earlier time she was actually scorned by many passengers as a slow, smelly, dirty vessel. They often voiced disdain when she showed up as a back-up boat for either of the faster and cleaner diesel vessels *Aucosisco II* or *Emita II*.

Then, in 1956, she got a reprieve. *Sunshine* went up on the rocks of Great Diamond Island in an early July morning fog and was a total loss. *Sabino* was backed out from her place at the head of the dock and "put into regular service" on the evening runs to Peaks Island.[32]

Short a vessel in the summer of 1957, the Casco Bay Lines management put *Sabino* on the day run to Bailey Island at the eastern end of the bay. Upon her late-afternoon return she made the familiar 4:15 p.m. trip to Little and Great Diamond Islands and Trefeathen Landing on Peaks Island. That summer *Emita II*, with Cliff Randall in the pilothouse, was the night boat to Peaks Island.[33]

"Bay Lines' officials have given no thought to retiring the old steamer because visitors select her for the all-day cruise to Bailey Island 'because she is so quiet in operation,'" claimed the *Portland Evening Express* in September of 1957.[34] This was more a public-relations statement than a reality. Visitors did not select *Sabino*. If

Sabino backing away from the dock at Portland in the 1950s. Note the dark spot above the center window. This is a result of tons of coal being loaded through this opening via a coal chute. (Jim Giblin Photo, MSM 91-12-226)

they wanted to go on the all-day cruise in the summers of 1957 and 1958, there was no choice; *Sabino* was the only vessel available. As noted, some passengers considered her dirty and objectionable. A dozen years later Bill Dunn would write in his *Casco Bay Steamboat Album*, "Because of her quietness underway, *Sabino* was one of the most popular excursion boats in the bay."[35] His statement is true of six percent of her working time on the bay, for she was an excursion boat only in her last two years. However, the romanticization of *Sabino* had begun!

Meanwhile, the Casco Bay Lines management was considering the disposal of their last, outmoded steam vessel. After a layup in the winter of 1957-58, her last regular use was in the summer of 1958. This was Cliff Randall's last summer as well, and both master and vessel went to the head of the dock that fall.[36] A new management in 1959 did put *Sabino* up for sale, and after three winters and summers lying idle at Custom House Wharf she was finally sold to "Red" Slavit of Haverhill, Massachusetts.

It was a sad day when the hose from the bilge pump siphoned water back into *Sabino*, resulting in an early-morning surprise for the Corbins. (Jim Corbin Collection)

CHAPTER 7

SABINO IN THE BAY STATE

AS AMERICA ENTERED THE turbulent decade of the 1960s, *Sabino* lay quiet and forlorn at the head of Custom House Wharf. Her last run had been in 1958 and there were no plans to reactivate her. The management of Casco Bay Lines offered the little steamer for sale, but it appeared that there was no interest in a 50-year-old steamboat. At one point, the tired old steamer was offered for one dollar to the state of Maine or the city of Portland.[1]

It was during these dark days of *Sabino*'s life that Captain William "Red" Slavit of Haverhill, Massachusetts, came along. Captain Slavit, or Red as he is known by all, is one of those bigger-than-life characters whom one encounters from time to time. He is accomplished in the arts of flying, boating, air-sea rescue and Yankee story-telling.* Red, who has long been Haverhill's harbormaster, began his boating career on the Merrimac River at an early age. "I started on the river when I was nine years old," remembers Red as he relates the story of his first boat. It was a "...little tin boat," with a one-cylinder Detroit, two-cycle engine. "The trouble...was...we didn't have that Schebler carbu-

retor. So I made a vaporizer out of a piece of pipe with holes in it and cotton batting and a one-drop oiler to drop the gas into the thing and we run it on that." It is doubtful that this arrangement would meet today's standards for flame arresters or environmentally correct fuel delivery, but it does attest to Red Slavit's ingenuity.

Red first saw *Sabino* in 1958 when he and two of his friends visited Portland. *Sabino* was moored at her usual spot and the three were looking her over carefully. A man came out of the little restaurant at the head of the pier and asked, "What do you think of that ship?" Red replied, "Ya, that's a nice steamboat." The man from the restaurant said, "That ain't a steamboat, they put diesels in all of them. The *Gurnet* and all of them been changed. That's a diesel." Red thought a minute and replied, "Well, I'll tell you what I'll do. There's three of us here, [so] I'll bet you three submarine sandwiches and three coffees

_____

*Red Slavit's accounts of *Sabino* are based on an interview conducted by the author and Rob Russell of Mystic Seaport on February 14, 1995 at Newburyport, Massachusetts. Red was 72 years old at the time of our visit.

that it's a steamboat." "Oh, I'm here every day…I know…I'll take the bet," replied the local. Red describes the result. "So he took the bet and we went down and there was the little steam engine in it and we got free sandwiches." It's a good thing they were right, because Red and his friends did not have a dime between them.

In 1961, Red and the two friends who liked submarine sandwiches were joined by a third colleague and returned to Portland. The purpose of this visit was to meet with Peter McLaughlin, President of Casco Bay Lines. Red describes the head of the steamboat company. "He had a derby hat on and a fancy suit with a fancy tie, a real dressed-up little guy with shiny shoes." Not being one to waste time, Red began, "Mr. McLaughlin, we'd like to buy that little steamboat." "Oh you would?" he said, "Well, I'd like to get rid of it. What will you pay?" "We can get you five hundred bucks," replied Red. "Well, you got a deal. Now what are you going to do? You got all these big rugged guys, are you going to carry it home?" Mr. McLaughlin raised his eyebrows when Red told him that they planned to take *Sabino* to Newburyport under her own steam.

Title to *Sabino* passed from Casco Bay Lines to William J. Slavit on March 14, 1961.[2]

Before leaving the safety of Portland Harbor, Red decided to have the soundness of the hull checked. This was also a necessary step in getting the old steamboat licensed to carry passengers, which was Red's ultimate goal. They brought *Sabino* to the Storey Marine Railway in South Portland and bored the hull planking. "All rotten," attests Red. His vision of reliving the steamboat days on the Merrimac suddenly evaporated.

Being a good Yankee trader, Red decided he should sell the aging steamboat right where she sat. He approached his friend Edward Lamb with the opportunity to own a steamer. The reply was short and to the point: "I don't want no steamboat." Not satisfied with this answer, Red presented a compelling argument–"Lammy, you gotta have a steamboat. Everybody's got one. You want to be an oddball without a steamboat?"

Thus was Lammy separated from $500 and Red relinquished title to the steamer to the new owner. As happens occasionally in life, Lammy immediately knew that he had made the wrong decision.

Edward Lamb enjoyed business success as owner of the American Armature Company in Danville, New Hampshire. He already owned a boat that he kept in Phil Corbin's Newburyport boatyard. Phil's son, Jim, remembers when Lammy bought *Sabino*. "He came down in his big Lincoln Continental full of fenders and ropes and steam pumps and whistles that he had taken off the *Sabino*." The collection of unusual paraphernalia attracted the curious, including Philip Corbin. The boatyard owner watched as the somewhat harried tenant unloaded his tarnished treasures. "Ya want to buy a steamboat?" Lammy asked.

Twenty-six-year-old Jim Corbin pointed out to his father that he had never even seen a steamboat, so the three were off to Portland. As soon as Jim saw *Sabino* laying at the head of the pier his mind was made up. Jim recalls, "I didn't even go aboard before I said, 'I want that.' " On April 19, 1961, Philip J. Corbin replaced the $500 that Lammy had relinquished to Red Slavit, and ownership of *Sabino* passed to the boatyard owner from Rings Island. Jim's elation was replaced by reality as he asked his father "How do we get this thing back to Newburyport?" They decided to make her as seaworthy as possible and steam her under her own power to her new Merrimac River home.

By now the local press had been alerted that the last steamboat in Maine was being sold. The *Portland Evening Express* lamented the sale, reporting in part,

"When the little steamer departs she will write finis to a once-brilliant chapter of maritime history. And hundreds of younger people who think now that a boat ride involves either the frenetic, hornet-like whine of an outboard or the noisy, shaking stench of a diesel may never know any better. They may never have the pleasure of hearing those soft sighs and chuffs and chuckles which are the only sounds a well behaved up-and-down steam job makes, or the clank of a furnace door, or the scrape of the fireman's scoop on wet steel plates, or the lordly stentorian blast of a real whistle."[5]

The plan to steam *Sabino* more than 75 miles down the coast was ambitious to say the least. A 53-year-old boat that had been inoperative for three years presented some interesting challenges to her crew. *Sabino* had been condemned by the Coast Guard's Office of Marine Inspection. Before they were allowed to leave Portland harbor, certain minimal work had to be accomplished to make the fragile old hull seaworthy and the machinery shipshape. Jim reports that "There was about a foot of steam cylinder oil and coal in the bilge all around the shaft. It was running in a tube of oil, six inches deep solid. We spent the better part of a week [just getting her clean.]" Of primary importance was the hull. The framing seemed strong enough but there were some questionable planks. The hull was patched up in South Portland with special attention being paid to her tender garboard strakes.

In preparing for the trip, the new owners solicited the assistance of Casco Bay Line's engineer Walter Clark. Engineer Clark is one of the unsung heroes of the *Sabino* story. Although he was known to vocalize disdain for the old steamboat, it appears that his true feelings were far more noble. The old engineer regularly visited Casco Bay's last steamer at the head of Custom House Wharf. He would check her machinery and the water level in her bilge. When the water level got too high, he would fire up the boiler and expel the bilge water overboard using the steam eductor in the engineroom. He would run the pumps and engine, and he would oil every part as needed. It is because of his diligence that the aging machinery is still operable today.

With the new owners, engineer Clark readied the boiler, engine, and auxiliary machinery and imparted enough knowledge to the neophyte crew to get them safely to Massachusetts. Although Walter Clark was too frail to make the trip himself, the Corbins managed to get an experienced steam engineer to accompany them. His name was Vic and he had served as a part-time engineer on *Sabino*.

Once the Coast Guard was convinced that these 1960s steamboaters had made the necessary repairs and had outfitted *Sabino* with all the proper equipment, they allowed the Corbins to depart. As Jim remembers, "We left at four o'clock one morning. [It was] a nice calm day, a beautiful day, and we started out of the harbor and we got just around Portland Light and we got into a southeast swell, then it went into about a six-foot chop and she started leaking."

Jim was in the pilothouse with his father and others, including Red Slavit. They were laying out a course for Newburyport. Vic was alone in the engineroom and the boat started slowing down. Jim ran down to see what the problem was. There was the engineer sitting in the port coal bunker, hugging a jug of wine and crying, "Turn around. We'll never make it." "He was scared to death," observes the younger Corbin. Jim took over the engineroom and began tightening pickings, because by now everything was leaking.

Red relates the adventure. "We started down the coast [with] filled fresh-water tanks. They busted open and we lost all the fresh water. So we pumped the ocean water to

When *Sabino* was sold to the Corbin family in 1961 she was a sad sight. Despite her outward appearance, she succeeded in making the trip from Portland, Maine, to Salisbury, Massachusetts, under her own steam. (Jim Corbin Collection)

The Corbins constructed a marine railway specifically for *Sabino*'s rebuild. Note the addition of a second whistle forward of the stack. (A. Loren Graham photo from the collection of Jim Corbin)

Sabino was a fine-looking boat once the Corbins had completed their restoration. This photograph shows one of the two new ventilators salvaged from *Emita* and installed to give symmetry to *Sabino*'s appearance. The ventilator on the port side is decorative and provides no air to the engineroom. (Jim Corbin Collection)

keep her going. We run her on salt to Newburyport. Terrible, but what are you goin' to do, you got no choice."

Red was correct on both points. Putting sea water into a boiler is a sure route to disaster. As the water evaporates, salt is left behind. The salt collects on the inside surfaces of the tubes, forming a hard crust that insulates them. This prevents the boiler water from keeping the tubes at a uniform temperature. Eventually the heat of the tubes rises to a point where the metal weakens and tube failure results. The alternative, letting the boiler go dry, is simply a faster way to reach the same point of disaster. Opting for the lesser of two evils, the novice engineers pumped water from the Atlantic Ocean into the 20-year-old boiler.

Red continues, "So we finally make it to Newburyport and tie it up…where the town big fancy pier is now." It was dusk, approximately 15 hours since the four-in-the-morning departure from Maine. It was another lucky episode in the life of a lucky little ship. After the high-adrenaline voyage from Portland to Newburyport, Jim was asked if he still wanted to have a steamboat. He replied, "Oh ya. I had all these visions of what I was going to do with it. It was a new challenge, something I hadn't done."

Now that *Sabino* was safe and sound in the Merrimac River, there was only one thing to do–run her. The Corbins delighted in steaming their new acquisition up and down the river, saluting all with the impressive resonance of her steam whistle. Their enthusiasm for the old steamer was shared by others all along the coast. But for all the attention and enjoyment of running the boat the reality was that there was much work to do before the Corbins could share the steamboat experience with others.

After each excursion on the river, the Corbins would confirm that the pumps were in place and running to be sure that the tired old steamboat would be floating when they returned. One day, this system fell apart when Charlie needed an extension cord.

Jim tells the story: "We had a hand who used to work for us, his name was Charlie. He was deaf. He just showed up one day like a stray cat in the marina. We took him in and he stayed with us for…18 years until he had to be put in a rest home." Jim's mother, Irene, continues, "He lived here. We traveled for eleven years and took him right along with us. He was just like part of the family."

Jim continues with the story of *Sabino*: "We had it in the water for about a year or two before we really started to do it over. She was leaking. She had garboard problems, so we had a sump pump on with a float switch. The boat was setting diagonal in the deepest part of the little bay we had there…with a couple of ropes holding her bow and stern…and it had a [power] cord running over [for] the pump."

Charlie would often take charge of the daily pumping of *Sabino*. On one occasion "…he saw the sump pump hose was tied to the rail on the after deck and the water was splashing on the rub rail. So Charlie untied it and he put it down in the water and tied it up again. So he's got it in the river now, and then he pumps the boat and he pulls the plug. Well, she started siphoning right back in. Being deaf he couldn't hear it.

"[There was] an inch and a half stream of water going in it. This happened early afternoon. Five o'clock the next morning my father's knocking at the door, "Jim, Jim, the *Sabino*'s sunk!" So there she was setting there on her side. 'Cause she had laid over. We ended up getting a diver. There was about three feet of water over the main deck at low tide.

"So we went aboard and got a cable across and we had a mushroom anchor made out of an I beam and

September 9, 1967, found hundreds of excited well-wishers on hand for the re-launching of *Sabino* following the five years of rebuilding and refinishing work done by the Corbins. (Jim Corbin Collection)

dropped over the edge of the cabin and ran a cable up and put a winch truck on in and we winched her up so she was…straight up and down. Then we put a cofferdam…up above the cap rail on the main deck and took some old mattresses and rags and stuffed the heads and we stuffed every opening…and we started pumping.

"We had five, four-inch pumps, two great big six-inch pumps, a fireboat and everything you could think of pumping, and we started the pumps one hour before the outgoing tide, low tide. When the tide started coming in and we were gaining but very little, we still had two-and-a-half, three feet of water over the deck and she was going down. But we realized that she was floating with two-and-a-half feet of water over the main deck. We had actually raised the…temporary sheer up so high that she was floating with two-and-a-half feet of water over the deck. Then all of a sudden, we got to a certain point she came right up and we had her running within two hours. We steamed her all down with her own steam."

Following the sinking, the Corbins resigned themselves to the fact that it was restoration time. Recognizing the enormity of the task, they decided that it would be best to build a marine railway dedicated solely to the *Sabino* project. The father and son team constructed their new railway next to Phil's house on Rings Island.

Sabino was set in a cradle that could roll in and out of the river with ease. Attached to the cradle was a shelter that provided protection for the boat and workers in winter months. The bow, stern, and smokestack protruded from the shelter, giving the entire affair the look of a Disney fantasyland creation. This arrangement allowed the Corbins to lower *Sabino* into the water to keep her hull planking swelled while they worked on sections above the waterline.

Jim started with the hull planking seams, and found that they were caulked with oakum and filled with a very hard seam compound. A worm shoe had been attached at some point but it had not been sealed to the keel. As a result the original keel was "…ate up with worm." The skeg was solid but showed a large number of worm holes as well. Deciding that there was enough good wood left in the keel and the skeg, the Corbins cleaned out all the soft spots and filled the holes with a hard cement caulking similar to what they had found in the seams.

They found the frames to be in good condition, but some of the hull planks had not fared so well. The garboard strake was replaced from the boiler aft. The sponsons were found to be loose and were repaired. Planking that was tight and intact was not disturbed, nor was it refastened. The Corbins believed in the old adage, "If it's not broken, don't fix it."

Conditions above the waterline were considerably worse. They found that the entire deck needed to be replaced. Recognizing the historic significance of the vessel, Phil and Jim took an approach of painstaking accuracy, replacing old wood with new wood in as close to replica form as possible. "I knew it was irreplaceable," says Jim. "I tried to be as exact as possible." In removing decayed portions of the boat, Jim cut cross sections through the old material. He would analyze each section and draw it out in detail on his drafting table. Then the skilled shipwright would make a replacement part and install it in the boat. "Every piece was put back exactly like original," reports Jim. This is the most time-consuming of any rebuilding approach, but it maintains the structure and design the original builders put into the vessel.

Jim describes the remainder of the project: "We replaced the decks, covering boards, deck timbers, and decided to do a complete restoration from the main deck up." The wood in the bulwarks was all replaced and the carving around the hawse pipe was duplicated. The stem piece, which had been extended to the upper deck by Casco Bay Lines, was removed and restored to its original height.

With the main deck complete, the Corbins turned their attention to the stanchions that supported the upper deck and the canopy. The originals were beyond repair so new ones had to be found. Irene describes the search. "I called all the way out to Canada to try to find some stanchions, eight feet long. You couldn't get anything over four." Phil responded, "The hell with them, I'll fix that." He built a twelve-foot lathe out in his workshop and cut locust trees from their own property. The Corbins turned 41 stanchions and installed them in *Sabino*.

One of the Coast Guard's concerns in certifying *Sabino* for passenger service was the height of the railings. Since her design in 1908, many regulations had changed to ensure the safety of passengers. One regulation required a higher rail than those that were currently on the boat. If the rails were raised to meet this requirement the boat would look awkward. Jim designed a rail that was attached to the locust stanchions behind the fore-and-aft benches on the foredeck. Continuing this design, he installed a bent-oak railing at the prescribed height on the stanchions on the stern of the boat. This was accepted by the inspectors and maintained a pleasing profile for the old steamer.

When *Sabino* arrived in Newburyport, her upper-deck railings resembled the siding of a railroad cattle car. The one-by-four boards laid up parallel to the deck may have met the letter of the law but they did nothing for her appearance. The Corbins replaced this with turned stanchions that supported a cap rail. Between the rail and the deck they fitted vinyl-covered storm fencing. The diamond pattern was similar to that of the original

rope lattice work and much more appealing to the eye.

To provide seating on the upper deck, the Corbins combined simplicity with function. In addition to their maritime interests, the Corbin family also operated a building wrecking business. One of their larger projects was the demolition of the Immaculate Conception Catholic Church in Newburyport. From the basement of the church came a number of wooden folding chairs that proved perfect for steamboat seating. Not only were they of the appropriate period for the boat but the morning routine of swabbing the decks was made considerably easier by the ability to fold and move the chairs.

The center supports for the canopy over the upper deck were galvanized pipe that by this time had rusted to oblivion. To keep this problem from recurring, the Corbins decided to deviate from original materials just enough to install stainless steel supports. The material at hand was rough-finished stock, so Jim chucked each piece up in the lathe and polished them to a proper shine prior to installation.

The only way to reach the upper deck at this time was by a steep stairway at the stern of the boat. Additionally, there was a stairway between the pilothouse and the stack that led to the top of the canopy. This had been installed during *Sabino*'s Casco Bay service to allow passengers to board from high piers at low tide. Jim replaced the canopy using one-by-four tongue-and-groove Alaskan cedar.

The greatest change in *Sabino*'s appearance during the Corbin restoration was the addition of stairways on each side of the pilothouse. In its original configuration, four steps afforded access to the pilothouse on the port side. When the pilothouse was raised and the upper deck extended to the bow, the route to the pilothouse required boarding the boat on the forward part of the main deck, walking through the engineroom to the stern, up the

Each morning, steamboat engineer Jim Corbin would push several wheelbarrow loads of coal down the long floating dock to fill *Sabino*'s bunkers. Low tide, such as seen here, made a difficult job even more challenging. (Jim Corbin Collection)

stairway, then forward the length of the deck. The Corbins saw a need for more direct access between the pilothouse and the foredeck. To accomplish this Jim decided to install stairways on each side. This design change was heartily supported by the Coast Guard and allayed their concerns about passenger access to exits. The aft stairway was also restored, thus giving passengers and crew three avenues of access between decks.

When the Corbins purchased *Sabino* there were more than 50 years worth of paint on parts of the boat. Jim reports, "She had paint a half-inch thick. You would go through the paint and there was no wood left." This problem was evident even in the engineroom. The railing was made from doubled up two-by-fours. Two-inch-wide sheathing extended from the rail to the deck on three sides of the boiler, but the area around the engine was open. Support for the railing was negligible and all the sheathing was bowed from years of strain.

Jim replaced the entire railing. The upper ends of the turned stanchions were set in doubled-up two-by-sixes that ran the length of the engineroom. Between each upright, the headers were cut with gentle arches, giving a pleasing line to the framework. Between the stanchions, a waist-high cap rail was installed on turned banister supports. This provided a safe separation between passengers and the mechanical spaces while allowing the curious to view the engineer as he attended to the details of his station.

The original after bulkhead in the engineroom was covered with diagonal planking to add strength. This provided mid-ship support for the upper deck. On this bulkhead were attached a beautiful set of ten-inch Ashcroft steam gauges. The bronze gauges indicate the pressure in the boiler, the vacuum or pressure in the low-pressure receiver, and the vacuum in the condenser. These were not original to the boat but came from the Massachusetts Electric powerhouse in nearby Haverhill, Massachusetts.

In addition to the gauges in the engineroom, Jim installed a very early Ashcroft pressure gauge in the pilothouse. This gauge predates the boat by some 50 years. Despite its age, it still provides the captain with a reasonably accurate indication of the boiler pressure. From this he can determine how powerful the reverse thrust will be when he rings a backing bell.

These gauges and much of the engineroom work came through the benevolence of John Clement. John hails from Northfield, New Hampshire, and is recognized as one of the elite fraternity of New England steam men. In his book, *The Steam Launch*, author Dick Mitchell describes John as "…an electrician, a carpenter, a plumber, a steam-fitter, a welder and a machinist."[4] John is just what the Corbins needed.

John began his work as a volunteer on *Sabino* shortly after she arrived in Massachusetts. When asked about the condition of the engineroom when he assumed the duties of chief engineer, John quietly replies, "It was fine. We just basically had to clean things up."[5] John's humility minimizes all the work and worry he and the Corbins put into shaping up *Sabino*'s engineroom. Jim Corbin speaks in the most laudatory terms of John Clement and his contributions to *Sabino*. "John bailed me out of about a million different problems," he says.

In addition to *Sabino*, the Corbins owned another steamboat, *Emita*. This veteran of Casco Bay was built in 1880 for the Catskill Lines at Athens, New York.[6] Like other Casco Bay steamers, she had been converted to diesel. In the late 1950s *Emita* was sold to a fisherman in Gloucester, Massachusetts, who wanted to use her replacement engine in his boat. The transplant had been completed when Phil Corbin arranged to purchase the unpowered hulk. *Emita* was towed to Corbin's yard by the fishing boat that had received her diesel engine.

Several parts from *Emita* were used in *Sabino* during the rebuild. When *Sabino* arrived in Massachusetts, she had square covers that fit over the coal bunkers as well as similar foredeck openings. Square covers on shipboard are not a good idea. If the cover is twisted while being removed or set in place it can fall through the opening. Only a circular cover cannot fall through its opening. The deck openings on *Emita* had been fitted with round plates. Several of these were removed from *Emita* and installed on *Sabino*.

Another *Emita* transplant was a pair of engineroom ventilators. These ducts carry fresh air to engine spaces on large ships where engineers and firemen are several decks below. *Sabino* and other small steamers have no need of these, as their enginerooms are open at deck level. It was not until late in her service on Casco Bay that a single ventilator appeared on the starboard side of *Sabino*'s stack. This single air funnel looked more like the bell of a sousaphone from the local marching band than the usual ventilators fitted to steamboats. At some point after their initial refit of *Sabino* the Corbins replaced this vent with two from *Emita*. When the two ventilators were mounted on either side of the stack, *Sabino* achieved a more balanced appearance. It is interesting to note, however, that the advantage of two ventilators is strictly visual. The port ventilator is mounted on the canopy with no opening to the engineroom below.

Philip's wife, Irene, provided the fine details of *Sabino*'s restoration. She installed red velvet curtains in the ladies saloon and matching carpeting on the deck. The ladies' head was fitted with an ornate oval mirror. These accouterments came from another Corbin demolition, the Strand Theater.

The restoration project planned to last one winter stretched into a five-year ordeal. To reassure their many well-wishers, the Corbins erected a sign that read, "PLEASE BE PATIENT! We are now completing restorations to have the steamboat *Sabino* in the water by mid-June."[7] With Murphy's Law still in effect, the gala re-launching took place on September 9, 1967. About 400 of the little steamboat's fans were on hand to share in the jubilation of the Corbin family as they launched her hot with the engine running astern and the whistle blowing.[8]

George Chard was the first captain of *Sabino* during the Corbin years, although Jim spent most of his time at the helm. John Clement was engineer and Bob Field of Byfield was fireman. Phil Corbin was the official greeter and anything else he wanted to do – after all, he owned the boat. Irene was the deckhand, then the purser, then the lunch counter waiter and the bartender.

The day started early when Jim would load coal one wheelbarrow at a time down the 500' floating walkway to the boat. There are about 14 wheelbarrow-loads to the ton, and *Sabino* held two tons of coal when empty. The Corbins received a donation of 70 tons of coal from the Newburyport power station – all they had to do was go get it. To retrieve the fuel, Jim was lowered into a manhole some 20' underground. There he would shovel the coal into a 55-gallon drum that was hauled up and dumped into a waiting truck. He didn't count how many of these barrels equals 70 tons, but it is more than he would like to know.

Each morning as Jim was bunkering *Sabino* he would be joined by his mother. Irene began her day by swabbing the decks from top to bottom, cleaning the carpet, shining the brass, polishing the mirror and scrubbing the toilets. Then she would return home, shower and make sandwiches to sell on the boat. During the day trips, Irene would sell the tickets, then climb aboard and sell candy and soda. On the longer evening excursions, she would sell her famous turkey sandwiches and tend bar.

The profits from the bar were an important part of the balance sheet when it came to paying the expenses of the operation, yet some patrons failed to understand this. On one charter a group of elderly ladies saw fit to bring their own bottles aboard rather than purchase anything from the bar. Jim relates the story: "We wondered where they were getting the mix from." He followed one of the patrons to the ladies' saloon and observed that she was diluting the jigger of spirits with tap water from the sink. Jim thought it better not to tell the passengers that this water was being pumped from the Merrimac River into the boat by a rusty old steam pump. "They thought it was great," smiles Jim. "In fact, I had to carry two of them off the boat bodily."

Sabino ran three trips a day and charters at night. For the occasions when music was planned, they carried an upright piano which could be rolled from its usual resting place in front of the boiler to the foredeck. Each Wednesday they featured a "Banjo Band," which Jim describes: "The band consisted of accordion, guitar, piano and a variety of other instruments." The only thing missing was the band's namesake instrument. Jim continues, "People never, ever complained about not having a banjo." *Sabino* ran two trips a night and they were booked ten weeks in advance.

The downriver trips to Haverhill were the longest excursions for *Sabino*. "This was 11 miles as the crow flies or 17 miles by water," reports Jim. There were several interesting sights, including the bridges that spanned the river. The first bridge was tall enough for *Sabino* to clear at any tide. The second bridge ran between Salisbury and Haverhill and connected Deer Island with the mainland. On the north span there was a swing bridge that was operated by a state crew. Although the bridge had been electrified for push-button operation, it never worked. Rather than fix it the state decided that the simpler course of action was to provide a crew to open the bridge manually on the infrequent occasions when a boat wanted to pass. The crew would walk around a capstan, pushing on long bars to open the bridge. They did not like providing this service so there was always a wait. The next bridge was in Rockville and it was also hand-operated but much faster to open. The Groveland Bridge was an electrified drawbridge and worked well. They would continue to Haverhill's Crescent Yacht Club, which was the head of navigation, and turn around. Three such trips were scheduled each year.

Like the former owners, the Corbins experienced draft problems with the boiler. It seemed to Jim that the problem was getting worse as the season progressed. When it reached a point where smoke was filling the engineroom, Jim decided he had to find a solution. Unbolting the access door on the side of the smoke box, Jim peered inside. There was nothing on the tubes that would restrict the flow of smoke, yet daylight could not be seen above the door. The only thing between the tubes and the top of the stack was the draft inducer. This ring of quarter-inch pipe certainly could not block out the sunlight. Jim reached up toward the inducer. He withdrew a handful of scorched feathers and some well-cooked seagull. The stack had become clogged with birds that had perched on the stack, become unconscious from the smoke, and fallen into the stack, piling up on the ring. Jim removed about 15 birds and the draft was improved dramatically. A screen on the top of the stack avoided repetition of the problem.

Sabino attracted volunteers young and old. Henry Woodward was a neighbor of the Corbins on Rings Island. Henry's three grandchildren, Alex, Livingston, and James, liked to help on the boat. When his work was done, James would sit on the stern of the boat and sing. Red Slavit came down one day and asked, "Jim, what are ya doing?" "I'm singing songs here." replied the young vocalist. Red snapped, "You'll never make a dime with that guitar. Throw it away. Tend to the boat, learn how to make money." Fortunately, the young man paid no heed to the old skipper and continued with his music. If he had listened to Red Slavit's advice we might never have enjoyed the music of James Taylor.

"For the first three years I never missed a single trip – night and day," remembers Jim. "We'd be done about midnight or quarter to one." They would let the fire go out at night and light off each morning after cleaning the ash pit and loading coal. Between the three day-trips and the two night-charters, they would bank the fire. After a few hours sleep, Jim would be back at it again.

In 1971, Jim returned home from a winter trip to Florida. Upon his arrival, Phil Corbin announced that he had sold *Sabino* to two men from across the river in Newburyport. The new owners were C. Bruce Brown and Joseph Pulvino. Bruce Brown was a city councilman in the city of Newburyport and Joe Pulvino was a former Newburyport resident and an aeronautical engineer. Jim followed his beloved steamboat across the river and became the third partner in SS Sabino, Incorporated. The corporate structure was Bruce Brown, President, Jim Corbin, Vice-President, and Joe Pulvino, Secretary-Treasurer.

Sabino was moored at Newburyport's Mercantile Wharf on Merrimac Street at the foot of Green Street. The steaming schedule for 1971 included weekday trips of an hour and a quarter at 1:00, 2:30, and 4:00, plus extended cruises at 7:00 and 10:00 p.m. on Wednesdays. The fare for the day trips was $1.75 for adults and $.75 for children. The three-hour upriver excursions cost $5.00 per couple or $3.00 per individual. The route for the evening trips was from Mercantile Wharf to the mouth of the river, then back upstream to Amesbury via the three bridges and return. This distance was 35 miles.[9] These longer Wednesday-evening trips were advertised as "Gay 90s Night" and featured a live band. For the majority of voyages, which had no band, music was piped throughout the vessel from an eight-track tape player located in the pilothouse. In addition to the rou-

tine sailings, there were special events such as the September 17 "Moonlight Cruise," which featured the "18 Harris Rock Band." The fare for that evening's entertainment was $6.50 per couple and $3.50 per single. Although the departure time of 8:00 p.m. is noted there is no mention of what time the rockers returned to Newburyport.

Following the 1971 season, Jim Corbin resigned from SS Sabino, Incorporated over professional differences. Brown and Pulvino continued operations the following year, promoting the old boat as "the last of the wood and coal [fired] steamboats" in the country. The schedule was much the same as the preceding year, but the long hours plus operational, maintenance, and regulatory demands began to discourage the two owners.

At one point, Coast Guard inspectors insisted that the reciprocating steam pumps be repaired because they were leaking steam and water from around the pump shafts. The owners tried to explain that this is how the rods were lubricated. Although this was good steam practice, the young inspectors were not persuaded, and the packings had to be taken up to a point well past that of prudent engineering.[10]

At this time, when SS Sabino, Incorporated was considering the little steamer's future, Mystic Seaport was looking for a historic vessel to carry passengers on river cruises from the museum. The combination appeared to benefit both parties and a one-year charter was arranged between the two. In 1973, SS Sabino, Incorporated entered into a lease contract with Mystic Seaport that would once again preserve this lucky vessel.

The Corbins operated *Sabino* on the Merrimac River from their home at Rings Island. Note the single ventilator next to the stack on the canopy. (Jim Corbin Collection)

Ahoy! Come take a Cruise on the

S.S. SABINO

BUILT IN 1908

LAST OF THE WOOD AND COAL STEAMBOATS

Summer Sailing Schedule

Day	Departure Times		
WEDNESDAY	1:30	3:00	4:30 P.M.
THURSDAY	1:30	3:00	4:30 P.M.
FRIDAY	1:30	3:00	4:30 P.M.
SATURDAY	1:30	3:00	4:30 P.M.
SUNDAY	1:30	3:00	4:30 P.M.

Adults $1.50 — Children under 12 $.50

MOONLIGHT CRUISE SATURDAYS 8 till Midnight

$6.00 per couple — Dancing and Refreshments

FOR RESERVATIONS OR CHARTERS CALL (617) 465-3473

Operating From

RING'S ISLAND
SALISBURY, MASS.

Approved and Inspected by
U.S. COAST GUARD

Capacity 100 Passengers

Sabino at Thames Shipyard, New London, Connecticut, in May 1973. Mystic Seaport shipwrights can be seen getting her ready for Coast Guard inspection. (Mary Anne Stets photo, MSM 73-5-171)

CHAPTER 8

NEW HOME–NEW HOPE

STEAMING FROM THE EAST into the sheltered waters of Fishers Island Sound, the first navigable river one encounters is the Mystic River. At its mouth is the village of Noank, renowned for its shipbuilding and boatbuilding, and approximately three miles up the river is the quiet community of Mystic, Connecticut. This picturesque New England village is shared by the towns of Groton on the west bank and Stonington on the east. It has long been a center of shipbuilding and marine-engine construction, and a favorite haven for sea captains, shipowners, and artisans of the maritime trades. Filling up 17 acres on the Stonington side of the river is Mystic Seaport, the renowned American maritime museum. Mystic Seaport was established in 1929 as the Marine Historical Association for the purpose of preserving America's maritime history, and its very appropriate site was formerly the shipyard of the Greenman brothers who launched sailing ships and steam vessels during much of the nineteenth century and into the twentieth.

In its early years, Mystic Seaport placed most of its emphasis on sailing ships, sailing fishing vessels, and yachts. During a meeting in the early 1970s, museum trustee Henry duPont pointed out to his fellow board members that the nineteenth century was equally an era of marine steam power, and observed that "…nowhere is there anything about steam in the collections of the museum."[1] The reply from the board was silence. Retired Mystic Seaport Watercraft Curator Don Robinson remembers what happened next. "We looked at each other and said, 'He's right…he's dead right.'"

A variety of suggestions emerged, none more tantalizing than the prospect of operating an authentic steam-powered vessel at the museum. An operating steamboat could provide visitors with an incomparable understanding of the power and mechanical intricacy of the age of steam. It would allow them to experience history rather than just have it explained.

Museum Shipyard Supervisor Maynard Bray knew of a small steamer that might fit the bill. The vessel's name was *Sabino*. Maynard and Museum Curator Revell Carr departed for Massachusetts on June 22, 1971, to have a look.[2] On the shore of the Merrimac River, they found the sole survivor of New England's fleet of many hundreds of steamboats. She was intact, surprisingly original, and still powered by her Noank-built engine. "There's the answer," Revell said quietly.[5]

Revell and Maynard met *Sabino*'s owners. "We planted the seed of our interest at this time,"[4] Revell says. Interest–in fact, enthusiasm–was accompanied by prudence. These wooden-boat enthusiasts were also wooden-boat realists. As much as *Sabino* evoked visions of silently steaming up and down the Mystic River, she also evoked visions of shipwrights replacing wood that had suffered the ravages of six decades.

The prudent decision was to enter into a one-year lease. This would allow all concerned to evaluate the impact of steamboat operations at Mystic Seaport. If *Sabino* could operate at a profit the Seaport would purchase her over the period of several years.[5] Another important part of the agreement was a survey of her hull and machinery.

Maynard remembers that part: "Executing the survey was my next duty. I hired Bill Lowell, Bath Iron Works' Chief Operations Engineer whom I had worked closely with while I was Chief Mechanical Engineer for that shipyard. I had a great deal of respect for Bill's knowledge of steam plants and figured I could do a cursory hull survey. Bill and I spent a day aboard *Sabino* and both furnished written reports as I recall. Our findings were that, although both hull and powerplant needed some work, the vessel was basically okay for the short term."[6]

By the terms of this agreement, the owners would operate the boat with deckhands and shore-side support provided by Mystic Seaport. The contract called for scheduled sailings each day during the summer season. Delivery was required by May 7, 1973.[7] All seemed to be ready except for one small detail–the 180 miles of open water that separated *Sabino*'s homeport from her port of summer embarkations. The 65-year-old veteran would have to make her longest voyage ever before she could go to work.

The master of *Sabino* at this time was Captain Dana Tirell, whose first encounter with *Sabino* was during his nine-year hitch in the U.S. Coast Guard. Boatswain's Mate Tirell was stationed in Portland for a time, and his cutter, *Coos Bay*, was moored next to the aging steamer. When SS Sabino, Incorporated was established, Captain Tirell came on as the full-time skipper. Unlike his predecessor on the Popham Beach line, Captain Tirell did not keep a shotgun in the pilothouse. He instead kept a trumpet he had played since his school days. It was not uncommon for a passing vessel to have a salute returned with a bugle call rather than the more traditional whistle signal. The *Amesbury News* reported the story of Dana Tirell and *Sabino*, describing him as the captain of the old steamboat and "…a right good captain too."[8]

There were two options for *Sabino*'s trip to Mystic. Option one was to steam her from Newburyport to Mystic, option two was to tow her. A decision was made to do some of both. *Sabino* steamed boldly out of Newburyport early on the morning of May 5, 1973, with Captain Tirell at the helm. Owner Bruce Brown and deckhand Bob Walton tended the lines while Joe Palvino took charge of the engineroom. Maynard Bray arranged to have Noank boatbuilder and Mystic Seaport friend Fred Cousins represent the museum on the delivery.[9]

The first leg was about 17 miles to the village of Annisquam on the west side of the Cape Ann peninsula. Here, Wilbur Roger's fishing boat, *Silver Star*, out of Salisbury, Massachusetts, took *Sabino* in tow. The tow continued all day as the two boats slowly made their way south past Boston and Plymouth on a heading for the Cape Cod Canal. As they approached the protected waters of the canal, engineer Joe Pulvino lit off the boiler. By the time they were in sight of Buzzards Bay, *Sabino* was under her own steam once again.

Arrangements had been made with the Massachusetts Maritime Academy on Buzzards Bay for the boat and crew to stay overnight. *Sabino* steamed to the dock and opened her doors. For the cadets, this was a rare opportunity to see the type of powerplant that had propelled maritime America into the twentieth century. For the senior members of the staff, it was a nostalgic trip to the days when they first had gone to sea.

Early the next morning, *Sabino* and *Silver Star* were once again underway. The heading was southwest toward Rhode Island and a bumpy ride through the waters around Point Judith. As the two small boats approached Point Jude, the sea began to rise. Soon the sound of tools hammering against the bulkhead filled the engineroom. Loose equipment and supplies slid across the deck. The rolling increased and the crew of four began lashing everything down while Captain Tirell gripped the wheel. The fact that *Sabino* was not under her own power added to the discomfort as she crashed through wave after wave. The seas increased and the tethered steamboat began to take water over the bow. The bilge level in the engineroom began to rise, but with no steam up *Sabino* could not run her pumps. Fortunately, Newburyport's fire chief had insisted that the crew take one of the fire department's gasoline pumps with them when they left Massachusetts. The fire pump kept the water in check as the boat and its occupants slammed through lumpy seas off Point Judith. Bruce Brown remembers that day: "We would have lost the boat if it weren't for that pump. I've never been so scared in my life."[10]

Slowly, as the boats made their way westward, the sea

The interior of the steam drum on the 35-year old boiler shows the effect of oxygen pitting. Although the boiler tested safe for operation, a new one was installed in 1979. (David Dodge photo, MSM 75-3-97)

began to subside. The comparatively tranquil waters of Fishers Island Sound were a welcome relief, and a less-preoccupied Captain Tirell called Mystic Seaport on the radio to announce their arrival. He was directed into the little harbor on Fishers.

"Instead of bringing her immediately up the river, I had arranged to lay *Sabino* against the fuel dock at Fishers Island for a few days while we cleaned her up and did some spring painting," Maynard Bray remembers. "Sprucing her up took many hands only a couple of days. Each morning, I loaded eight or ten shipyard guys aboard the Seaport workboat *Two Brothers* (now Chris Cox's *Nimble*) and ran over to West Harbor – loaded with brooms, scrub brushes, pails, detergent, vacuums, scrapers, paint, and brushes. We really worked the old girl over and greatly improved her appearance."[11]

On Tuesday, May 8, 1973, *Sabino* departed Fishers Island. She steamed two miles across Fishers Island Sound and was met in Noank by an excited crowd.* As New London's newspaper, *The Day*, reported: "Boarding her at Noank for the maiden trip upriver were President Daniel B. Fuller of the Mystic Chamber of Commerce, Mystic and Noank Fire District officials, Groton town councilors, Stonington selectmen, and Seaport Director Waldo C.M. Johnston, and other guests and staff members."[12] In all, approximately 30 exuberant supporters were on board for the occasion.

Members of the Steamship Historical Society of America were among the guests on *Sabino*. Bill Ewen, Jr. reflects on that day's voyage, describing the transit as "ghosting up the river." However, he is quick to point out that the tranquility of steam travel was suddenly and frequently punctuated that day by a cannoneer who fired salutes from the foredeck of *Sabino*. The saluting gun crew was none other than Mystic Seaport's Director of Ship Preservation, Don Robinson.

At the Route 1 highway bridge in the center of Mystic, Captain Tirell blew down to the engineroom on the speaking tube and gave the word to engineer Palvino. "Let 'em know we're a steamboat!" He barked. Obediently, Joe tossed a quart can of oil into the firebox. The resulting plume of smoke delighted the jubilant crew, but may have raised the eyebrows of downtown neighbors.

Sabino had arrived at Mystic on schedule and in fine style, but before her first scheduled run there was work to be done. *Sabino* steamed to the Thames Shipyard at New London and was hauled out of the water.* The weakest structural members were tended to first. Suspect planks were inspected and repairs were made as required. Butts and seams in the hull planking were caulked below the waterline. All the work on *Sabino* was completed to the standards of the U.S. Coast Guard. "The real highlight of the whole operation was the relationship with the Coast Guard," Don Robinson recalls.[13] The government inspectors accepted a four-year restoration plan that would bring *Sabino* to top running condition. However, *Sabino* was allowed to operate each year following an interim inspection to ensure that she was safe to carry passengers in restricted waters.

Steamboat operations the first year consisted of seven trips daily from a temporary landing north of the New York Yacht Club building. The first six were half-hour trips departing at half past the hour from 11:30 on. At 7:00 *Sabino* departed for a two-hour downriver excursion to the mouth of the Mystic River.

---

*As mentioned earlier, Noank was home to the company that built *Sabino*'s powerplant in 1908. Unbeknownst to anyone aboard, a circuit had been completed as *Sabino* glided past the site of her engine's creation some 65 years before.

*Mystic Seaport's lift dock was still under construction at this time.

During this first season, the new museum attraction averaged 2,900 passengers every week, and the season ran until the end of October. This long schedule provided visitors and crew with a wide range of experiences. In the dog days of summer, passengers would complain when the only seats left were those in the torrid engineroom. As the days grew shorter and the leaves began to fall, passengers would complain because there were not enough seats for all in the warmth of the engineroom.

More than 30,000 passengers enjoyed a cruise into history as they relaxed aboard *Sabino* that summer and fall, and listened to the quiet music of her machinery and the clang and jingle of her signal bells. The experiment was a success and *Sabino* found a new home. All the museum had to do now was pay for her.

Organizations such as Mystic Seaport fill an important role in the preservation of history. And fortunately organizations such as Mystic Seaport attract a cadre of generous benefactors who give freely of time and money to ensure that the mission is fulfilled. Some of the museum's most significant funding quietly appears in time of need, and so it was with *Sabino*.

One of Mystic Seaport's benefactors was John Deupree of Cincinnati, Ohio. Mr. Deupree had been an admiring passenger on *Sabino* during her Popham Beach years, and as a supporter of the 1973 charter experiment, he was elated by the success of the venture. During a conversation with Frank Kneedler, the Museum's head of development, John asked if anyone had come forward with an offer to pay for the boat. Frank lamented that no one had. "I'll supply enough money. How much is it?" Frank informed him that the price tag was $75,000. John said, "Then I'll supply the port half." Elated by the offer, Frank gratefully accepted and began to look for the other half of *Sabino*'s funding. Three weeks passed with no significant progress toward financial support for the balance of the boat. "Has anyone bought the starboard half?" John asked when the two next met. "Well, no," admitted Frank. "Well, Jean will buy the second half." Frank smiled. John Deupree had just offered his wife's support for the purchase of *Sabino*.

As testimony to their generosity, two brass plaques are mounted on the rear of *Sabino*'s pilothouse. They read as follows:

Each ship and building at Mystic Seaport represents a specific period in time. It is not always the year the exhibit was built, because structures evolve to meet changing needs. Houses are often enlarged to meet the demands of an expanding family. In the restoration process it may be decided to portray the period of the enlargement rather than to remove and discard antique building materials in an attempt to return to the original design. The period depicted by the restoration tells the story of one stage in the building's development but still allows a return to its original structure.

Ships are modified to accommodate changes in cargo or the waters they sail. Changes in rig are common. Representing any one period in the evolution of a vessel is most appropriate; like the house, it can tell the story of how it changed to meet the demands of a different trade or any other circumstance. *Sabino* has undergone several changes since she was designed in 1908. So apparent are the modifications that photographs of the boat can be dated with accuracy based on the structural and accouterment changes. Such minor details as the color or the name boards can place the date of a photograph within one or two years.

Major differences, such as pilothouse location, reshaping cabins, and the addition of an upper deck, are structural changes not easily modified. Other considerations such as the two forward ladders between the upper and lower decks are present-day requirements of the Coast Guard for passenger safety. These cannot be removed if the intention is to carry passengers for hire. The obvious and reasonable decision was to represent *Sabino* as she was when she arrived at Mystic Seaport. She is a composite[14] vessel that has evolved to meet the needs of different assignments. A restoration plan was devised that would allow major structural work to be accomplished each winter and also allow the boat to operate each summer.*

Careful documentation of the project was maintained from the outset. Written descriptions of materials, procedures, and work completed were kept by project leader Robert W. Morse. Robert Allyn prepared detailed drawings that documented original construction as well as renovation. The results of this latter effort are a complete set of accurate *Sabino* drawings,* many of which are reproduced here.

While decisions were being made for the restoration of the hull and superstructure, the needs of the engine-room were obvious. The first *Sabino* engineer at Mystic Seaport was David Dodge. In his engineering report addressing the 1973-74 season he makes the following observations: "When the *Sabino* finished the 1973 season it was in bad mechanical condition; three of the four steam pumps weren't working at all. The grates were held up by a fieldstone and a cement block in the ash pit. The piping was marginal. That winter I found that the steam line to the inoperative bilge pump had holes in an elbow that you could see light through. Makeshift repairs were to be found almost anywhere one looked."

From time to time in the world of engineering an attempt to solve a serious problem delivers a humorous result. Dave Dodge knew that he had to get the residual oil out of the boiler. The oil had entered the system when excessive lubrication of the pumps was the only way to keep them running. Dave decided to fill the boiler with Tide detergent and allow it to soak. He felt that a low fire

*The story of *Sabino*'s restoration could be a volume in itself. The details of the work completed between 1975 and 1980 are found in the "The Restoration/Reconstruction of the Steamboat *Sabino*." Robert W. Morse, the shipwright in charge of the restoration, compiled this document, and copies are on file at Mystic Seaport. We will attempt only to document the highlights of each year's restoration work here.

*These drawings are available from Mystic Seaport's Ships Plans Department

would aid in circulating the water through the boiler tubes. As a persuasion against building a head of pressure, he tied the whistle valve open. The unexpected result was a flood of soapsuds emanating from the whistle and cascading over the decks and the adjacent dock.

Dave reports that two sets of boiler tubes had been replaced during the summer and that the overall condition of the tubes was poor. The Almy Boiler Company of Providence, Rhode Island, had manufactured the boiler in 1940. Dave noted in his log that, "Almy made an informal offer last winter to rebuild the boiler with welded tubes for $7,000."[15] Dave's log continues. "It was decided that over the winter I would work on the pumps and everything else would be dealt with in the spring. I was the only one working on the boat until June. If we had been working in April the way we were in June we would not have been so late."[16]

Dave made several necessary and prudent changes to the boiler. He replaced ball valves on the mud drums with approved "Everlasting" blow-down valves. He replaced the gauge glass fitting with one of proper design. New safety valves were installed when the company rebuilding the old ones reported that they were beyond hope.

One part of the report touches on the Gordian knot of wiring. The battery-charging system was a unique challenge. "There seems to be a good deal of confusion about how the battery chargers work. The system consists of three 12-volt batteries connected to three 12-volt, 10-amp automotive battery chargers. Both Jim Giblin and Bill Watson said this couldn't work. It does."[17] Oh, the mysteries of steamboating.

The litany of problems found and problems solved is a testimony to the tenacity of *Sabino*'s first Mystic Seaport engineers, Dave Dodge and Jack Cawley. Suffice it to say that they accomplished much and had much still to accomplish.

MYSTIC SEAPORT, MYSTIC, CONN.

VIA

STEAMSHIP SABINO,

North & South along the Mystic River

SEVEN STEAM TRIPS A DAY

DEPARTING EVERY HOUR ON THE HALF HOUR

MONDAY 11:30, 12:30, 1:30, 2:30, 3:30, 4:30 7:00 (later in season)
TUESDAY 11:30, 12:30, 1:30, 2:30, 3:30, 4:30, 7:00 (later in season)
WEDNESDAY 11:30, 12:30, 1:30, 2:30, 3:30, 4:30, 7:00 (2-hour trip to Noank)
THURSDAY 11:30, 12:30, 1:30, 2:30, 3:30, 4:30, 7:00 (2-hour trip to Noank)
FRIDAY 11:30, 12:30, 1:30, 2:30, 3:30, 4:30, 7:00 (2-hour trip to Noank)
SATURDAY 11:30, 12:30, 1:30, 2:30, 3:30, 4:30, 7:00 (2-hour trip to Noank)
SUNDAY 11:30, 12:30, 1:30, 2:30, 3:30, 4:30, 7:00 (2-hour trip to Noank)

TICKETS issued for all trips may be purchased from **TICKET PURSER** next to New York Yacht Club

NO SEAPORT ADMISSION REQUIRED FOR 4:30 & 7:00 CRUISES
SPECIAL CHARTER RATES AVAILABLE TO ORGANIZED GROUPS: CONTACT *SABINO* AGENT (203) 536-2631, MYSTIC SEAPORT

This was the first schedule for *Sabino* during her Mystic Seaport years. (Flyer from the author's collection)

Bob Morse (beard and hat), the head of the restoration effort, watches Jim Polk wash the boat down. (Kenneth E. Mahler photo, MSM 75-12-44)

CHAPTER 9

MYSTIC SEAPORT—A STEAMBOAT COMPANY

SABINO WAS HAULED on the lift dock on May 30, 1974. With the operating season so close at hand, the crew hoped to accomplish enough "temporary" repairs to pass the Coast Guard's scrutiny. Without a certificate of inspection, *Sabino* could not carry passengers for hire.

Those who have owned wooden boats know that there is no such thing as a simple project. The immediate repairs stretched into weeks of work. June slipped past as shipwrights and engineers worked diligently to meet the safety requirements of the Coast Guard. The Fourth of July celebration was held without a steamboat. *Sabino* was unceremoniously lowered into the water on July 5. A leak immediately developed in the area of the fire pump through-hull fitting. The boat was hauled and the area was repaired in less than an hour. Again, the boat was launched.[1]

On July 10 *Sabino* passed Coast Guard inspection for all hull and deck requirements. Ten days later the engineering inspection was held, but the results were not good. The fire pump and the air pump failed to work properly. Finally, on July 29, the sonorous blast of *Sabino*'s whistle announced that she was once again on the river. After a few adjustments the boat and crew settled into a summer routine. The log entry for August 9, 1974 reads, in part, "Finally got onto a regular schedule."[2]

The year 1974 also marked the first season with Captain Howard E. Chapman as the regular captain of *Sabino*. Captain Chapman, or "Chappy" as he was known to all, was a good-humored mariner with 32 years experience to his credit when he arrived at Mystic Seaport. In a 1976 interview, Chappy offered his thoughts about *Sabino*. "*Sabino* is the most unique ship I've ever been on, and I'm proud to be her captain. I'd like to run her as long as I'm able to."[3] Chappy served as *Sabino*'s master until his death.

By September, everything seemed to have settled down. Ridership totals were low due to the late start but Chappy and the crew enjoyed the season. "Not much money, but lots of fun," reads Chappy's log for September 19, 1974.[4] *Sabino* logged only 71 underway days that season with a total of 15,037 passengers. Much work was needed to bring the aging steamer into top condition, and to ensure a full operating season. Although her thorough

Robert Morse was in charge of *Sabino*'s restoration at Mystic Seaport. Here he carefully checks the details of the new keel being installed in 1975. (J. Deupree photo, MSM 76-1-111)

Palmer Watrous is shown here pouring babbitt main bearings in *Sabino*'s 68-year-old engine. This bearing metal is composed of copper and tin and can be poured at a temperature of 800 degrees Fahrenheit. (J. Deupree photo, MSM 76-3-150)

The main cabin was rebuilt in 1978. The amount of work accomplished during the winter months is impressive when one realizes that *Sabino* was back in service in May. (Kenneth E. Mahler photo, MSM 78-12-71)

restoration would begin a year later, significant structural work began in November 1974.

The weakest structural members were replaced first. The stem, keel, and sternpost had never been replaced and they were well past due. The rudder post and rudder box were removed carefully to provide the necessary details for reconstruction. Patterns were constructed from the original materials and new structural members were installed. New knees were attached to the sternpost to replace the deteriorated originals. Forward of the sternpost, a ten-foot section of keel was renewed.

In the engineroom, progress was being made on a number of fronts. The steam gauges that came with *Sabino* were of questionable accuracy. The gauges inform the engineer about pressure at various points in the system, and by interpreting these gauge readings the engineer makes adjustments to the boiler, engine, and pumps to operate the boat properly. This can only be accomplished if the gauges read true.

The three engineroom gauges indicate the main boiler pressure, the pressure or vacuum in the low-pressure receiver, and the vacuum in the condenser. Each of these gauges was built by the Ashcroft Gauge Company, which is now a subsidiary of Dresser Industries. Dresser was contacted and agreed to overhaul the gauges for the museum. Joseph Weiss of Dresser reported that "They looked awful after being subjected to the elements and salt water for so long. But they were in fine working condition. All we did was polish them up and recalibrate them. Our charts on them proved that those gauges are

Peter Vermilya was responsible for the restoration of *Sabino*'s pilothouse. Earlier modifications such as fiberglass trim was replaced with more traditional materials. (Mary Anne Stets photo, MSM 78-4-81)

still as accurate as any gauges manufactured today."[5]

The 1975 season started on May 10 and ran for 124 days. During this period, 31,166 passengers enjoyed the sights and sounds of the Mystic River from the decks of *Sabino*. Although she had served nobly for yet another season, the senescent steamer was still in need of extensive restoration.

When restoring a wooden boat, starting at the beginning often means starting at the bottom. The initial plan was to get the area below the waterline in sound condition. The restoration report for 1975-76* provides the following details. "The *Sabino*'s keel showed extensive repairs done over the years. It presented a loosely held-together composite of long and short layers which represent these repairs. A replacement of almost the complete keel was needed.

"The stern post showed advanced deterioration due not so much to rot as to a break-down of the wood structure. It probably was the original stern post and most certainly a major contributor to the leaks known to originate in this area. The stem was also in very poor condition.

"Much of the planking below the waterline needed to be replaced. The fastenings were in poor condition and their holding power was almost non-existent. There was a great deal of checking in many cases completely through the planks, and in some areas large flat areas had spalled off. The inner corners of the plank seams had been broken off through repeated caulking over the years. Ninety percent of this planking seemed to be original. Further caulking would not be able to be driven tight because of the condition of these seams.

"The sponsons' chine logs were known to be sources of leaks and the seams on the lowermost sponson planks were in the same condition as the hull planking seams."

Before work could continue, years of accumulated oil, coal dust, and ash had to be removed from the bilge. This

*There was no hull restoration work completed during the winter of 1974-75 because the *Charles W. Morgan* was still on the lift dock.

was accomplished by removing the garboards and emptying the hull from below. Many garbage cans full of this black, viscous mix were removed with great care to avoid dropping any into the river.

The hull was supported with double rows of shoring that were cross-braced to prevent distortion as the keel was removed. An additional line of shores was placed at eight-foot intervals along the rub rail for added stability. The old keel was cut into short lengths with a chainsaw and split out in pieces. The old sternpost was carefully measured and the angle of the shaft hole determined before it was removed. Frames 30 through 32 (transom frames) were completely replaced along with the horn timbers. The old engine beds were removed and new ones of yellow pine were installed.

A hatch was installed in the saloon deck to allow an emergency exit for engineers. New stem, apron, stem knee, and gripe pieces were made of white oak and installed. The collision bulkhead that once marked the forward end of the crew's quarters was replaced. The sponsons received new chine logs. Fifty percent of the planking and fastenings below the waterline were removed and replaced. Thirty-six frames were either replaced or repaired.

Ten men worked on the hull throughout the winter and succeeded in getting *Sabino* in operating condition for the 1976 season. May 29 was the premier voyage for America's bicentennial year. Captain Chapman and engineers Dave Dodge, Don Albert and Edward Gilman kept everything running smoothly. The summer deckhands tended the lines and the brass polish to ensure an attractive and safe vessel for more than 53,000 passengers that season. The operating year ended on October 31, 1976.

Winter work for 1976-77 focused on the supports under the boiler and makeup tank. These areas were two of the most difficult to access for maintenance and repair. As a result, they had been ignored for years. A different approach was taken for each space. To replace the makeup-tank flooring, the tank was first removed. This allowed shipwrights easy access to rotten members and allowed enough room to replace them without unnecessary scarfing.

Starting at the bottom and working to the top is the sequence in boat restoration. Here the new canopy is lowered into place for the 1980 operating season. Seven years after her arrival at Mystic Seaport, the major restoration work on *Sabino* had been completed. (Mary Anne Stets photo, MSM 80-3-200)

While this work was underway, preparations were made to lift the boiler. Long timbers spanned several deck beams to distribute the weight over a large area. Heavy cribbing was erected on either side of the boiler with a ridgepole spanning the two piles. A chain hoist was attached between the pole and the boiler. The entire boiler was suspended above the engineroom deck, and this afforded enough space to remove the old boiler bed. Framework was built under the hanging boiler and concrete was poured into the form to a depth of four inches. Once the concrete cured, the form was removed and the boiler returned to its original location. Adjustments were made for pipe alignment to the boiler and then everything was reconnected.

A log entry for May 29, 1977, records the first operating day of the season. Each captain is required by law to maintain a log of the ship's daily activities. Weather conditions, arrivals and departures, observations and events are all part of the permanent record of each vessel. Reading a ship's log provides historic information and occasionally humorous insight into daily steamboat operations. Chappy offers the following vignette. "Mad man got upset about *Sabino* leaving him on dock. We were three minutes late. He threw two cups of coffee at us. Had security handle case."[6]

Another interesting entry that year shows the tribulations of steamboats as well as the creative problem-solving skills of the captain. The log for August 9, 1977, shows a departure for the downriver trip at 1809. Three minutes later the 90-minute cruise was abruptly terminated. The entry reads, "Engine broke down. Had to be towed to SB/D (steamboat dock). Went to Seamen's Inn for a loan to pay off passengers."[7]

Operations ceased for the year on October 30. The 1977 season saw 53,188 passengers on *Sabino*.

In the fall of 1977 a cradle to hold *Sabino* was constructed on the lift dock. While this work was being done, the canopy, pilothouse, and stack were removed from the boat. The dock and cradle were lowered into the Mystic River and the steamboat was floated into place. The entire assembly was lifted out of the water. *Sabino* in her cradle was slid on greased planks into the main shop of the DuPont Preservation Shipyard. Once in place, the main deckhouse was separated from the hull and suspended above it.

This was accomplished by jacking the entire boat high above the floor. Long beams were inserted through the windows of the house and attached to opposite walls of the shop in steel holding brackets. The deckhouse was detached from the hull and the hull was lowered, leaving the house suspended above it. This provided workers with approximately four feet of clearance between the two parts of the boat.

The restoration report reads: "The decking was cut away in several places to allow inspection of the deck beams and other foundations. It was already apparent that the deck had lost its crown…some frames and ceiling planks were obviously in need of replacement. However, when the deck beams and tops of the sponsons were seen, it became obvious that we would need to retop the vessel as well.

"As it turned out, having to retop the *Sabino* meant that we had about double the work of a normal retopping since the vessel's sponsons had been added to the outside of the hull and then the tops tied into the old hull, with the deck."

The first work undertaken was the replacement of single-sawn frames in the sponsons. The main beam and several beams forward of it were then installed. Once these were in place, the shape of the hull could be maintained while the deteriorated frames and planks of the forward half of the hull could be replaced. The upper two thirds of almost every frame in the after 40' of the hull needed to be replaced. Half of the ceiling planks were also renewed.

The entire stern of the boat was replaced. Following the usual practice of framing a fantail stern, a series of heavy timbers was cut to the shape of the stern, scarfed, and bolted together. This was connected to the hull by the planking, horn timbers, and frames. When the stern was completed, the remaining deck beams were installed. The opening for the engine and boiler was framed in. Four hatches providing access to the sponsons, auxiliary machinery space, and makeup tank were located between the deck beams. New coal bunkers were constructed and lined with 18-gauge galvanized sheet metal. When the framing was complete, the deck was laid, caulked, and painted.

While several shipwrights worked on the hull others worked on the pilothouse. In his report, Peter Vermilya

Sabino's boiler was disassembled into four pieces for removal in 1991. Cleaning of the watersides showed deterioration in the mud drums. Both drums were replaced. (Mary Anne Stets photo, MSM 79-4-10)

Lowering the rebuilt boiler through the upper deck. Manufacturer's identification can be seen lettered on the new mud drums at the bottom of the boiler. (Nancy d'Estang photo, MSM 92-3-168)

documents the progress and procedures used in the restoration. He reports that the sills and floor were completely replaced and that the exterior sheathing was 95 percent replaced. On the roof, fiberglass moldings were replaced with new ones of yellow pine.

Peter reported an interesting change to the pilothouse. "A wedge-shaped section was taken off the bottom of both post and siding 3" deep at the front of the house and tapering down to 0" at the after end, such that the entire attitude of the house is tilted forward relative to the old position."[8] This corrected the appearance of the pilot looking "uphill" as the boat moved forward.

Robert W. Morse, project leader for the restoration, continues: "The main house was set down on the deck and fastened with metal 'L' clips which were bolted to the stanchions and lag-screwed to the covering board. This was a temporary measure to allow the vessel to be put back in service for the 1978 season."

Sabino was moved out of the shop, launched, and refitted with her canopy, stack, and other accouterments. The efforts of 13 skilled workers had her ready for service the first week in June.

Following the 1978 operating season, *Sabino* was once again moved into the main shop. The goal for this year was restoration of the main house.

All sheathing was removed from the exterior of the deckhouse and replaced. Rail stanchions along the main house were replaced first, with oak studs installed next. Every beam on the passenger deck was also replaced. The sides of the main house were sheathed with v-joint,

Some of the wood replaced during the 1991-92 winter's work is believed to be original to the boat from its construction in 1908. (Nancy d'Estang photo, MSM 91-12-276)

The rebuilt engine is lowered into the engineroom. Although the engine's weight is far less than the crane's capacity, seeing the 84-year-old engine hanging far above the river was an anxious moment for those who worked so closely with the machine. (Photo by the author, author's collection)

Positioning the boiler inside the engineroom. New wood under the boiler and engine required modifications to piping and realignment of critical components of the propulsion plant. (Nancy d'Estang photo, MSM 92-5-209)

tongue-and-groove cypress. The interior sheathing of the main house was removed, as it was not original. It was replaced with v-joint tongue-and-groove cypress. The entire main house was covered with a new deck of cypress over white oak beams, which in turn was covered with canvas and sealed. Attention was then directed to the heads. Both were sheathed with 2" cypress, as was the partition between them.

The jubilation that accompanied *Sabino*'s substantial rebuilding was tempered by the sad news that Captain Howard E. Chapman had passed away. A collection was taken to purchase a memorial barometer and clock for the pilothouse.

The search for a new captain soon followed. The successful applicant was Captain Richard Lotz. Dick came to Mystic Seaport with an extensive maritime résumé that included marina management, charter-boat operations, and yacht deliveries. The variety of boats that Dick had encountered during his career was impressive, yet it lacked the unique challenges of a "bell boat."

be doing both) and two bells to run astern. Attached to the center of the wheel frame in the pilothouse is a third bell-pull. This one is connected to a small jingle bell, resembling an old screen-door bell, which is attached to the engineroom bulkhead next to the gong. The "jingler" can signify more speed, finished with engines, or stand by for bells depending where in the sequence it is rung.[†]

Dick took to the boat immediately and his skills as a boat-handler were exemplary. He was comfortable with *Sabino*'s heavy displacement hull and he artfully directed the vessel through its every move. He admits however, that it took a little time to gain the confidence that when he sounded a bell signal "…something's going to happen." Dick describes the relationship between the captain and the engineer as a simple agreement. "I don't sink the boat and he doesn't blow up the boiler." The arrangement has worked fine so far.

Sabino was moved out of the shed in April 1979 and launched. The pilothouse was installed and the old canopy put back in place. Through the efforts of 20 Museum staff and volunteers, *Sabino* was ready for summer operations in May. In the fall of 1979 *Sabino* did not make her annual trip into the shipyard's main shop. For that year, the partially renovated steamboat remained in the water as work on a new canopy commenced in the main shop.

While extensive work was being completed in the engineroom, Gary Adair made new rope netting to replace the diamond link fence that had been installed by the Corbins in the 1960s. (MSM 92-6-103)

Since the first day of *Sabino*'s service on the Damariscotta River, her engineers have received their orders via an archaic system of bells and jingles. The bell is a large, twelve-inch gong mounted on the bulkhead directly over the engine.[*] The captain has bell-pulls on both the port and starboard sides of the pilothouse that allow him to strike the gong through a series of chains, cables, and pulleys. The code is one bell for ahead or stop (you can't

---

*The current engineroom gong in *Sabino* is larger than her original. It came from a retired Portland steamer named *Radium*. This boat was so named because of her cost. When the owner got the final bill he named his new boat after the most expensive metallic element known at the time.

[†]In my research, I have uncovered nine different bell codes for steamboats. The bell code used on *Sabino* is an abbreviated bell system with no "slow down" bells in the code. It appears that as long as captain and engineer agree, any bell-code system will work.

Sabino coming around the bend toward the dock.

A platform was built in the shipyard shed and a series of L-shaped blocks were fastened across the edge of this platform at the location of the new deck's edge. The new canopy was constructed on this frame. Stringers and deck beams were assembled, with careful attention being paid to the camber and sheer of the canopy. Next, the framing for the stack and the ventilators was installed. Cypress was again used for the decking as it had been in other areas of the boat. Like the deck below, the canopy was covered with canvas and sealed. The assembled roof was moved to the dock on a trailer and lowered into place with a crane. A new flagstaff, six feet longer than the old one, was stepped into place at the rear of the canopy.

In addition to the four shipyard staff that worked on the canopy, the artisans in the small-boat shop built a new 12' tender and installed it in a cradle atop *Sabino*'s canopy. New life-jacket lockers were built and installed on the exterior sides of the passenger cabin. Finally, a new whistle was installed in *Sabino*. This three-chime Crosby is thought to have come from the tug *Westerly*. It was a gift from George Utter. This whistle is of the proper pressure range for *Sabino*, and replaced a steam locomotive whistle that had gone to sea.

The season of 1980 marked the end of this first major restoration of *Sabino* at Mystic Seaport. As with all wooden boats, the work is never really done. Each year, maintenance work, modifications due to regulatory changes, and improvements for safety and daily operation are on the little steamer's schedule. Coast Guard inspectors are quick to point out suspect pieces of wood, and defective sections are replaced as needed.

In 1991 one inspector speculated about the condition of the frame ends under the engine. That year, shipwrights investigated the suspect framing and determined that it would be prudent to replace it. To get to the frames, the engineroom had to be cleared of all machinery. First, the stack and canopy were removed, then a hatch was cut in the upper deck to gain access to the engineroom from above. This modification returned the upper-deck structure to its original configuration. The boiler, engine, pumps, and makeup tank were removed by crane through the new opening.

While shipwrights worked to install new wood in the hull, *Sabino* engineers worked on the boiler and engine. The boiler was acid-cleaned to remove years of accumulated scale on the watersides. As expected, this cleaning excavated problem areas in the boiler. The result was the replacement of the mud drums.

There is no record for when *Sabino*'s engine was last rebuilt. We know that the low-pressure cylinder was rebored during the Damariscotta years. There is also evidence that the high-pressure cylinder was sleeved at some point in her long career. We know that the main bearings had been repoured in 1979. Although the engine was running reasonably well in 1991, the fact that we had to remove it for hull repairs seemed to provide an ideal opportunity to rebuild the engine.

The engine was disassembled in the Museum's weld shop and shipped to Reno Machine in Newington, Connecticut, where the cylinders and steam chests were bored true. A new high-pressure piston was constructed to match the oversize cylinder. New valve faces and new rings were installed throughout. The main bearings were found to be out of alignment and new babbitt was poured. The bearings were align-bored to assure accuracy and the engine was returned to Mystic for reassembly. Foundry patterns for the crosshead slippers were made and new pieces cast at the Mystic River Foundry. The new pieces were machined at the museum and installed in the engine. All clearances and tolerances were in compliance with accepted marine applications found in Osborne's *Marine Engineers Manual*.

Part of the work being completed in the hull was replacement of the engine bed. The skilled shipwrights were so accurate in their work that only a .060 inch sheet of copper needed to be installed under the entire engine to bring it into perfect alignment with the shaft. The makeup tank was painted inside and out, and the pumps were adjusted and repacked before being lowered into the hull. Then the rebuilt engine and boiler were carefully lowered into place. During this rebuild all remaining asbestos was removed from the boat by professionals.

Sabino began the 1992 season a little later than hoped, but it was worth the wait. The boiler steamed well and the engine ran with quiet precision. As an added bonus,

Sabino as she appears in the Mystic Seaport service. (Nancy d'Estang photo, MSM 91-7-12)

there was a noticeable reduction in the amount of fuel consumed.

Shortly after the engine rebuild the Steamship Historical Society of America chartered the boat for its annual meeting. The engineroom was crowded with enthusiastic members as *Sabino* slipped silently downstream toward Noank. When the boat cleared the Mystic River railroad bridge, the engineer opened the throttle for full speed. Spectators stood three deep at the engineroom railing. The engineer looked up from the throttle station and stated, "Someone up there is wearing a Rolex watch." Everyone looked around as one or two members looked at their watches. Eyeing one of the Rolex wearers, the engineer quipped, "Sir, would you please turn down your watch, I'm having difficulty hearing my engine." The appreciative audience roared with laughter.

The *Sabino* season of 1992 was both happy and noteworthy. In addition to the work completed in the engineering spaces, *Sabino* achieved status as a National Historic Landmark. The United States Department of the Interior bestows this honor on structures of national significance. A bronze plaque mounted on the door between the foredeck and the engineroom proudly proclaims the following:

S. S. SABINO
HAS BEEN DESIGNATED A
NATIONAL HISTORIC LANDMARK
THIS VESSEL POSSESSES NATIONAL
SIGNIFICANCE
IN COMMEMORATING THE HISTORY OF THE
UNITED STATES OF AMERICA
1992
NATIONAL PARK SERVICE
UNITED STATES DEPARTMENT OF THE INTERIOR

The complete story of the steamboat named *Sabino* is not contained in this volume because the story is not over. It moves forward with each day and with each visitor to Mystic Seaport.

We at Mystic Seaport are the current stewards of *Sabino*. It is our duty to preserve her for future generations. The work of the shipwrights in the 1970s was not the last restoration of the aging steamer. It was simply the most recent one.

The responsibilities of stewardship are formidable. In accepting this charge we have committed ourselves to keeping this venerable old steamboat in the best physical and mechanical shape–and keeping her steaming. In doing this, we must maintain a balance between the originality of the boat and the needs of daily operation. We must evaluate each change for its appropriateness, making changes for the sake of the vessel rather than the ease of the crew.

In meeting contemporary regulations of the Coast Guard we have attempted to keep the boat looking as original as possible. When a new valve must be installed, we replace the modern valve handle with an antique one. We avoid using modern ball valves although they are legal and faster to use in operation. We avoid using stainless steels, aluminum, and plastics that would detract from the appearance of the boat. We compromise nothing in safety, but challenge ourselves to find ways to integrate modern safety features into the historic ambiance of the vessel. By adhering to a high standard of authenticity, we often find that we also enjoy the operational simplicity of a bygone era.

Sabino is the last of her kind. She is a legacy from our past and an important link in our history of going on the water. Through her operation, tens of thousands of Mystic Seaport visitors can share an experience that is available nowhere else in the country. They marvel at the silence of the engine, they are wary of the heat of the boiler, and they wonder at the simplicity of this 90-year-old technology. It works today as it did in 1908.

With continued diligence *Sabino* will serve for generations to come. This is our charge.

The author on duty in *Sabino*'s engineroom. (Claire White-Peterson, MSM 94-6-9)

THE DAILY ROUTINE

THE DAILY ROUTINE on a steamboat is not as much a matter of course as it once was. Since *Sabino* is the last of her kind, recording the unceremonious activities of her crew here will avoid creative speculation later.

The crew consists of a minimum of one licensed captain, one licensed engineer, and two deckhands. On most occasions, an assistant engineer is also on watch. The schedule is flexible, but the goal is to have a clean, fully provisioned boat ready to leave the steamer dock at 11:00 am daily. Any of the crew can be male or female and we have had both in most jobs over the years. For the sake of simplicity, I shall use "he" in describing the day's work.

0730 – Deckhands arrive. The first task is to fill the boiler makeup tank which is under the foredeck. This requires the addition of approximately 195 gallons of water daily. The tank is filled with a garden hose. A second hose is used to fill the potable water tank mounted on the canopy.

Next are the pump-outs. The holding tank for the heads and the bilge are pumped using two separate systems. The holding tank water ends up in the city sewage system. The bilge water is pumped to an oily water separator. This machine separates the oil from the water. The water goes into the city sewage system. The oil is collected throughout the summer and then sent out for recycling at the end of the season.

The pump-out procedure can be accomplished either by pumps on board *Sabino* or ashore.

One deckhand places a canvas cover over the engine and shovels the ashes out of the boiler ashpit. Ashes are first shoveled into a 10-gallon pail and then carried to a wheelbarrow ashore. They are dumped in the bucket of a loader that in turn empties them into a dumpster.

He then covers the boiler grates with wads of newspaper. It takes about 50 full sheets of newsprint to cover the grates. The deckhand then loads one wheelbarrow full of kindling – usually pine, fir, cedar, and other woodshop scraps – on top of the paper. He then sweeps the engineroom deck.

Next comes several wheelbarrow loads of coal. It usually takes seven loads of approximately 120 pounds each to fill the port bunker. Each bunker holds about two tons of coal. A day's steaming will burn between 800 and 1,000 pounds of fuel. While the coal is being loaded, a second canvas cover is hung in the engineroom to minimize dust on the working parts of the engine.

The other deckhand starts the morning wash-down. First the canopy is scrubbed. The upper deck comes next. To clean this deck properly, the folding chairs are closed and moved aside. The two long deacon's benches remain in place. The treads of the forward and after stairways are likewise scrubbed.

The ship's bell is hung in its place on the pilothouse. A 48-star national ensign is run up on the flagstaff.* The *Sabino* pennant is run up on the jackstaff. The public address system microphone is connected and attached to the holder on the rear of the pilothouse.

Once the coal has been loaded, the canvas covers are removed and stowed. The main deck is swept and scrubbed. The railings, seats, and lateral surfaces are cleaned and the windows and doors are opened.

0830 – The engineers arrive. First on their agenda is reading the previous day's log entries. They then begin polishing the brass and lubricating the machinery. The brass on the bulkhead (gauges, clock, signal bells, pipes, etc.) and the boiler fittings are polished on alternate days with the brass on the engine and in the engineroom. The engine, pumps, and other moving parts are lubricated. The oil sump under the engine is pumped out.

*Each vessel at Mystic Seaport flies an American flag (National Ensign) that represents the period to which it had been restored. The restoration plan for *Sabino* established that she would be represented as a composite. A decision had to be made as to which of several American flags would be appropriate for display on the new acquisition. Since the most significant change to her appearance had been the addition of sponsons in 1927, it was decided that a 48-star flag would be flown to represent that era.

0915 – The engineers check the water level in the boiler and makeup tank and light the fire. It takes 15 to 20 minutes to see pressure on the gauge. While pressure is coming up the engineers align the valves and fire the boiler as necessary. When pressure reaches approximately 50 psi, the engineer blows down the boiler. This lowers the level in the boiler while discharging solids left behind from the city water.

The engineer then bars the engine through at least one full revolution. Next, he opens the throttle valves and starting valve to warm the engine. When the temperature of the engine is hot enough and the gauge pressure exceeds 80 psi the engineer begins to rock the engine back and forth on steam. When all condensate has been worked through, he runs the engine astern. This wears the moving parts on their "reverse" side and forces water past the keel condenser to keep it cool.

While the engineers are preparing to get underway, the deckhands shower and change from their deck-cleaning clothes to their deckhand clothes, usually a *Sabino* uniform shirt and shorts. When they return, they put a block of ice in the icebox and begin polishing the brass on deck and in the pilothouse.

At 1000 the captain arrives. He activates the electrical circuits for the depth finder and the radio. He reads the log and checks with the engineer to be sure that everything is ready for the day's work.

The first trip is at 1100. *Sabino* departs the steamer dock and proceeds north to the basin behind the Stillman Building where we turn south. As we turn, a deckhand begins a narration describing some of the museum exhibits. We steam to the highway bridge where we turn again and return to the steamer landing. It is the engineer's responsibility to make the half-hour ride last 30 minutes. To accomplish this, the engineer runs the engine at about 60 rpm. The half-hour rides depart on the hour between 11:00 a.m. and 4:00 p.m. At 5:00 *Sabino* departs on a 90-minute cruise from the museum to the mouth of the Mystic River and return. Despite radio communications between the steamboat and the bridges, we often must wait for either the railroad bridge or the highway bridge to open. This makes the 90-minute time for the cruise a minimum rather than a guarantee. In July and August *Sabino* also makes a 90-minute downriver cruise at 7:00 p.m.

On many occasions throughout the summer *Sabino* is scheduled for charters. These are usually two-hour trips between the hours of 7:00 and 9:00 p.m. Charters are often enjoyable for the crew, as there is a more festive atmosphere than the tranquil public trips downriver.

In addition to the routine for the trips, the engineer must run the oily water separator in the separator shed. This machine separates the bilge water from any oil it might contain. The water goes to the sewer and the oil is retained to be recycled at the end of the year.

The engineer analyzes the boiler-water chemistry every other day. He adjusts the boiler chemistry daily to maintain proper levels of pH, phosphates, chlorides, sulfites, and dissolved solids.

Once the passengers have disembarked, the captain can leave for the day. The deckhands empty the trash, remove the bell, lower the flags, secure the lines, connect the power lines, and call it a day.

Every other day, the engineers blow the soot from the boiler tubes with a steam lance. Each day they must stay aboard until the boiler is filled with water, the fire is out, and the pressure is down to 20 psi. When this is all accomplished, they check the stern tube and bilge level, secure the lights and lock the doors on their way out. The clock often indicates 10:00 p.m. as the engineers head home.

TECHNICAL DATA

Hull: Length overall – 57'½"
Maximum beam – 21' 11½"
Maximum draft – 6' 3"
Length between perpendiculars – 53'½"
Station spacing 5.304

Speed : 8 knots

Boiler: Almy sectional water-tube boiler

Type "Z," three-drum

Grate area – 16.5 sq. ft.

Steam drum – 14" seamless
Mud drums – 3" seamless

Generating tubes – 1"
Schedule 80 threaded pipe

Heating surface – 545 sq. ft.

Weight – 1,095 lbs.

Engine: James H. Paine & Son, Inc. Two-cylinder, inline
compound
High-pressure cylinder – 7"
Low-pressure cylinder – 14"

Stroke – 12"

75 Indicated Horsepower at 150 psi (gauge)
at 200 rpm

Shaft: Intermediate shaft – 3" steel
Tail shaft – 3" Tobin bronze

Screw: 48" diameter by 54" pitch
Four-blade, right-hand rotation, bronze
Slip – 25%

Wet air pump – Worthington type VA duplex
steam 3 x 2¾ x 3

Boiler feed pump – Worthington duplex
steam 4½ x 2¾ x 4

Fire pump – Worthington duplex steam 4½ x 2¾ x 4
(can be used for emergency boiler feed)

Bilge pump – Warren duplex steam 4½ x 2¾ x 4

Injector (boiler feed) – Metropolitan 5-N, ¾" pipe

Gauges – Ashcroft 10"-diameter, bronze case
Boiler pressure – 0 to 200 psi
LP Receiver – Compound 30" hg. to 30 psi
Vacuum – 0 to 30" hg.
Boiler pressure (pilothouse) –
Ashcroft 6"-diameter open center 0 to 180 psi

Electrical: 12-volt DC from lead-acid battery with
National-Pyle turbine belted to Motorola alternator
for charging underway

APPENDIX 3

SABINO'S PROPULSION PLANT

THE CYCLE

The steam plant consists of several devices arranged so that the water and steam go through a complete cycle. (Fig. 1) A fire in the lower section of the *boiler* converts water into steam. Since the boiler is an enclosed vessel, steam pressure rises as more heat is added until pressures in excess of 100 pounds per square inch are obtained. The steam then leaves the boiler via the main steam line and enters the engine through the throttle valve. This valve controls the amount of steam admitted to the engine and thus regulates its speed. The energy in the steam moves the pistons up and down as it travels through the engine. The expanded steam leaves the engine from the low-pressure cylinder exhaust port and passes through the *feedwater heater* on its way to the *condenser*.

When water is converted into steam, one cubic inch of water expands into approximately one cubic foot of steam. When the steam is condensed back into water, the

decrease in volume results in a partial vacuum in the condenser. This vacuum is used to pull on one side of the low-pressure piston as the steam pushes on the opposite side, thus helping to propel the boat. The

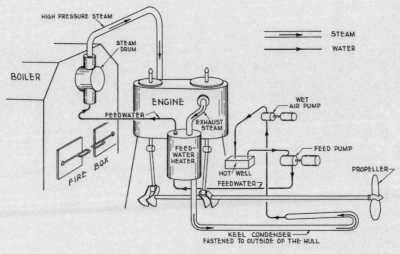

FIGURE NO. 1

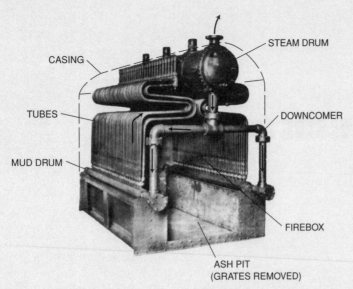

CASING

STEAM DRUM

TUBES

DOWNCOMER

MUD DRUM

FIREBOX

ASH PIT
(GRATES REMOVED)

BOILER—CASING REMOVED

THE BOILER

Steam is generated in a coal-fired Almy *watertube boiler*. In a watertube boiler, the water is heated as it flows through a multitude of tubes that are exposed to the heat of combustion. The steam rises through the water and is collected in the *steam drum* at the top of the boiler. The water level in the boiler is critical and can be observed in the *gauge glass* on the front of the steam drum. This glass not only shows the level of the water in the boiler but it also allows one to observe that steam is completely transparent. (Fig. 2) A gauge on the engine room bulkhead indicates the boiler pressure. Two *safety valves* allow steam to escape from the boiler if the pressure gets too high. These safeties are set at 140 and 145 pounds per square inch.

THE ENGINE

The engine in *Sabino* is a 75-horsepower Paine two-cylinder compound engine. "Compound" means that it is a two-stage engine that uses the same steam twice.

Steam from the boiler enters the high-pressure steam chest where it is alternately distributed to the top and bottom of the *high-pressure (HP) cylinder*. In the cylinder, the steam acts upon the piston forcing it to the end of its stroke. Once there, the direction of the steam flow is reversed, pushing the piston to the opposite end of the cylinder. Steam remaining on the non-powered side of the piston is exhausted from the HP cylinder to the *low-*

amount of vacuum in the condenser is indicated on the vacuum gauge on the engineroom bulkhead (wall.)

The *wet-air pump* pumps the water, and any air that has leaked into the system, out of the condenser. The water goes into the *hotwell* and the air is exhausted to atmosphere. The water in the hotwell is then pumped through the feedwater heater and into the boiler by the *boiler feed pump*. The feedwater heater uses the exhaust steam from the engine to raise the temperature of the water entering the boiler. This saves fuel and reduces the shock of cold water entering a hot boiler.

Steam jets have been installed in the boiler above the fire to aid in complete combustion of the bituminous coal that fuels *Sabino*. These jets reduce smoke output by approximately 80%. The jets, however, consume a lot of steam and this loss must be made up in the form of make-up water from a tank in the bow of the boat.

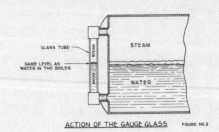

GLASS TUBE

SAME LEVEL AS
WATER IN THE BOILER

STEAM

WATER

ACTION OF THE GAUGE GLASS   FIGURE NO.2

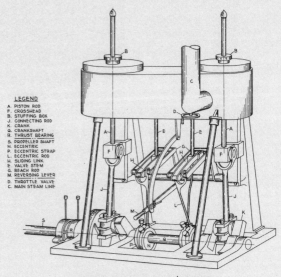

LEGEND

A. PISTON ROD
F. CROSSHEAD
B. STUFFING BOX
J. CONNECTING ROD
K. CRANK
Q. CRANKSHAFT
R. THRUST BEARING
S. PROPELLER SHAFT
N. ECCENTRIC
P. ECCENTRIC STRAP
L. ECCENTRIC ROD
W. SLIDING LINK
E. VALVE STEM
M. REVERSING LEVER
G. REACH ROD
D. THROTTLE VALVE
C. MAIN STEAM LINE

PRINCIPAL PARTS OF SABINO'S ENGINE

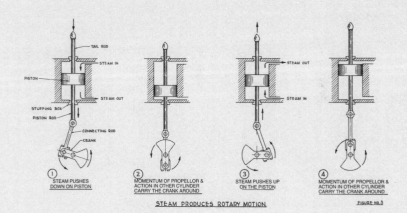

STEAM PRODUCES ROTARY MOTION

① STEAM PUSHES DOWN ON PISTON

② MOMENTUM OF PROPELLER & ACTION IN OTHER CYLINDER CARRY THE CRANK AROUND

③ STEAM PUSHES UP ON THE PISTON

④ MOMENTUM OF PROPELLER & ACTION IN OTHER CYLINDER CARRY THE CRANK AROUND

FIGURE NO. 3

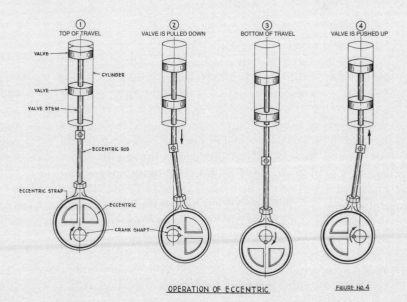

① TOP OF TRAVEL ② VALVE IS PULLED DOWN ③ BOTTOM OF TRAVEL ④ VALVE IS PUSHED UP

OPERATION OF ECCENTRIC

FIGURE NO. 4

pressure (LP) steam chest where it is distributed to the LP cylinder in a similar manner.

The reciprocating motion of the piston is transmitted through the bottom of the cylinder by a *piston rod*. This rod is attached to a crosshead. This is the point where the reciprocating motion begins its transition to the more useful rotary motion. The *connecting rod* completes the link between the crosshead and the *crankshaft*. The crankshaft is connected to the *intermediate shaft* that in turn is connected to the *tail shaft*. The propeller, or *screw*, is attached to the end of the tail shaft.

Opposite the *piston rod* is a *tail rod* that protrudes through the top cylinder head. The motion of the piston can be observed by watching the reciprocating movement of the tail rod above the engine.

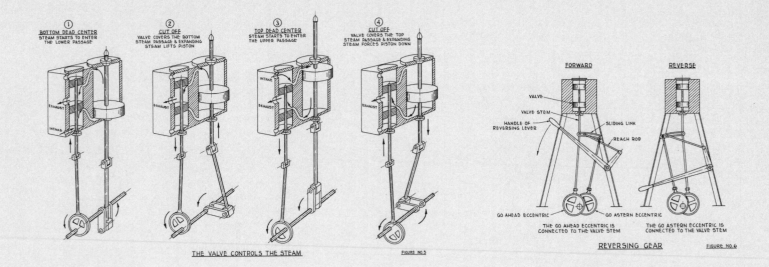

① BOTTOM DEAD CENTER
STEAM STARTS TO ENTER
THE LOWER PASSAGE

② CUT OFF
VALVE COVERS THE BOTTOM
STEAM PASSAGE & EXPANDING
STEAM LIFTS PISTON

③ TOP DEAD CENTER
STEAM STARTS TO ENTER
THE UPPER PASSAGE

④ CUT OFF
VALVE COVERS THE TOP
STEAM PASSAGE & EXPANDING
STEAM FORCES PISTON DOWN

THE VALVE CONTROLS THE STEAM   FIGURE NO.5

FORWARD   REVERSE

VALVE
VALVE STEM
HANDLE OF
REVERSING LEVER
SLIDING LINK
REACH ROD

GO AHEAD ECCENTRIC   GO ASTERN ECCENTRIC

THE GO AHEAD ECCENTRIC IS
CONNECTED TO THE VALVE STEM

THE GO ASTERN ECCENTRIC IS
CONNECTED TO THE VALVE STEM

REVERSING GEAR   FIGURE NO.6

EXPANSION

Conservation of steam results in the conservation of water. The ability to minimize water consumption is important, especially on vessels traveling in salt water. One effective means of conserving steam is to cut off the flow of steam to the cylinder before the piston reaches the end of its stroke. Steam continues to exert a force on the piston even after live steam no longer enters the cylinder. This expansive property of steam allows the engineer to cut off the flow of steam approximately one third of the way through the stroke and thus save a great deal of water and fuel. The expansion results in lower pressure and a cooler temperature of the steam as it exits the HP cylinder and enters the LP. This pressure of the steam acting on the LP piston can be observed by watching the compound gauge on the engineroom bulkhead.

VALVES AND VALVE GEAR

Piston valves control the admission and exhaust of the steam to and from the cylinder. These spool-shaped valves are connected to *eccentrics* by a *valve rod* and an *eccentric rod* An eccentric is a disc of cast iron that is attached to the crankshaft. The hole to accommodate the crankshaft is off-center–eccentric–to the outer circumference of the disk. This off-center location of the hole causes the eccentric to rotate in an oval path rather than a circular one. A cast iron strap, which is free to rotate on the eccentric, communicates the motion of the eccentric to the rods. It is the motion of the eccentric that controls the motion of the piston valves in the steam chest. The motion of the valves opens and closes steam passages, and this allows the steam to enter and exit the cylinder.

REVERSING

It is essential that marine engines be reversable. The mechanism that accomplishes this is called a *valve gear*. The Paine engine in *Sabino* uses what is called a Stephenson Link valve gear. This system employs two eccentrics. One eccentric times the valve to allow for clockwise rotation of the engine causing the boat to move forward. The other results in counter-clockwise rotation that moves the boat astern. Since two separate eccentrics control the valve timing, a steam engine will operate equally as effectively in either direction.

GAUGES

The pressure at various points in the steam cycle can be observed by watching the gauges on the engineroom bulkhead. The top gauge indicates the boiler pressure, which is approximately the same as the pressure operating on the HP piston. The gauge on the port side of the bulkhead is a compound gauge that registers the pressure or vacuum in the LP receiver. The gauge to the starboard side is a vacuum gauge. This indicates the vacuum in the condenser. The pressure gauges are graduated in pounds per square inch while the vacuum gauge is graduated in inches of mercury (as is a barometer.) The compound gauge indicates pressure to the right and vacuum to the left and is graduated in pounds per square inch on the pressure side and inches of mercury on the vacuum side.

THE CONDENSER

As steam is exhausted from the LP cylinder, it first passes through the feedwater heater and then to a brass pipe on the outside of the hull. This pipe is the *keel condenser*. As the exhaust steam enters this condenser it is cooled by the surrounding river water. When sufficiently cooled, it becomes water. Since approximately one cubic inch of water can be heated into one cubic foot of steam, the inverse occurs during the condensation process. This results in a vacuum in the condenser. The power of this vacuum is used to pull down on the opposite side of the LP piston as explained earlier.

HOTWELL

The water from the condenser is pumped into the hotwell where it is stored until enough has accumulated to be pumped back into the boiler. The hotwell is an open tank located on the port side of the engineroom behind the feedwater heater. In addition to its function as a temporary storage vessel, it also provides a means by which impurities can be separated from the water before it goes into the boiler. The hotwell is divided into three compartments. The water from the condenser, called condensate, is pumped though a charcoal filter that removes the cylinder lubricating oil from the water. The water then enters the forward-most compartment of the hotwell. In this chamber any remaining oil is collected on luffa sponges that are suspended on the tank. The second section of the hotwell allows any solids to drop out of the condensate. The third compartment holds the cleaned water that lifts a float valve as it accumulates. Once the float valve rises sufficiently, it admits steam to the boiler feed pump that pumps the water from the hotwell to the boiler via the feedwater heater.

THE BELLS

Sabino is a bell boat. There are two bells located on the engineroom bulkhead. The captain in the pilothouse rings these bells to inform the engineer as to what speed and direction he wishes the boat to go. The large gong located above the pressure gauge is the primary signal. One gong when at rest means run the engine slow ahead. When running, one gong means stop. Two gongs means run the engine slow astern. After an ahead bell, the smaller "jingle bell" may be rung to indicate that the captain wishes more speed. After a stop bell, the "jingler" means finished with engine. After the engine has been stopped the jingler means stand by to get underway.

If *Sabino* is proceeding in a forward direction and the captain wishes to run astern, he first rings one gong for stop, then two gongs for astern, followed by a jingle if he wants more speed. This is the usual sequence of bells to stop the boat when approaching the steamer landing.

The abbreviated bell code used on *Sabino* does not allow for any "slowing" bells. As a result, when the captain wishes to go from full ahead to slow ahead he must ring one gong for "stop" and a second gong for slow ahead. There have been a great variety of bell codes used on steamboats through the years. As long as the captain and the engineer agree on the code, any system can be used effectively.

THE ENGINEER

In responding to the bells, the engineer uses two basic controls to operate the engine. The *throttle valve* regulates the amount of steam entering the engine and the *reverse lever* controls the direction of the engine and the point of cut off for the steam. *Sabino*'s engineer must also tend the fire, shoveling approximately one-half ton of coal per day. This controls the rate of combustion by regulating the amount of air entering the boiler from under the grates. He monitors the water level in the boiler and controls the addition of make-up water through valving to the feed pump and by what is called an *injector*. The injector is a device that uses the steam in the boiler to propel a stream of water into the boiler. In case of a failure of the boiler feed pump and the injector, the engineer can use the fire pump and an emergency *boiler feed*. The engineer also lubricates the engine and pumps, keeps the engineroom shipshape and answers questions from passengers on board.

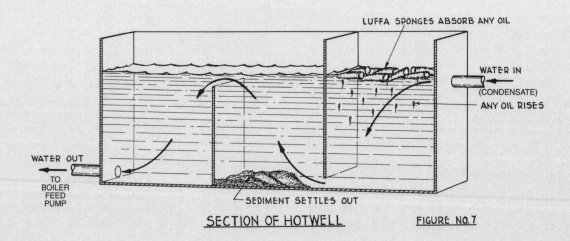

SECTION OF HOTWELL   FIGURE NO. 7

NOTES

CHAPTER ONE

1. U.S. Department of Commerce, *Merchant Vessel List.* (Washington, D.C.: U.S. Government Printing Office, 1908).

2. Jane Sugden, ed. and Norman Kotker, *New England Past* (New York: Harry N. Abrams, Inc., 1981), 147.

3. John A. Garraty, *The American Nation* (New York: Harper & Row, 1966), 523.

4. Sugden, *Past,* 147.

5. Herbert G. Jones, *Sebago Lake Land* (Portland, Maine: Bowker Press, 1949), 35.

6. George Foster and Peter Weiglin, *Splendor Sailed the Sound* (San Mateo, California: Potentials Group, Inc. 1989), 18.

7. John Ives Sewell, "Steam Boat Days at the C.C.I.A." *C.C.I.A. Notes* (Christmas Cove, Maine: Christmas Cove Improvement Association, undated), 1.

CHAPTER TWO

1. Constance Rowe Lang, *Kennebec, Boothbay Harbor Steamboat Album* (Camden, Maine: Down East Enterprise, Inc., 1971), 35.

2. Advertisement, *Boothbay Register,* 16 May 1908.

3. Ibid.

4. Harold W. Castner, "The Damariscotta Steamboat Company." *Lincoln County News,* 11 September 1947.

5. Byron M. Boyles, "The Damariscotta River Steamboat Company." *Steamboat Bill,* August 1947, 32.

6. U.S. Department of Commerce, *Annual Report of the Supervising Inspector-General, Steamboat-Inspection Service.* Fiscal year ending 30 June 1909, 139.

7. Lang.

8. Castner.

9. Castner.

10. Ibid.

11. Boyles.

12. Castner.

13. Boyles.

14. Castner.

15. Boyles.

16. Ibid.

17. *Marine Engines and Machinery for Yachts, Passenger Boats and Tugs,* advertising brochure from James H. Paine & Sons, Inc. Noank,

Connecticut, circa 1907.

18. *International Marine Engineering*, April 1908, 53.

19. *Marine Engineering*, October 1897, 40.

20. Boyles.

21. *Boothbay Register*, 6 June 1908.

22. Castner.

23. Boyles.

24. Ibid.

25. Paine, *Marine Engines.*

26. Castner.

27. Boyles.

28. "Compound Marine Engine." *Marine Engineering*, July 1902, 372-73.

29. Castner.

30. Ibid.

31. Ibid.

32. Boyles.

33. Castner.

34. Ibid.

35. Ibid.

36. Ibid.

37. Ibid.

38. Harold W. Castner, notes in the Castner Papers. Skidompha Library, Damariscotta, Maine.

39. Castner, "Steamboat."

40. Ibid.

41. Floyd Clymer, *Henry's Wonderful Model T* (New York: Bonanza Books, 1955), 134.

CHAPTER THREE

1. John Ives Sewell. *CCIA Notes* (Christmas Cove Improvement Association, Spring 1966).

2. Bill Caldwell, "Harvey F. Gamage, Master Shipbuilder, South Bristol, Maine," *Down East*, April 1976, 43-45.

3. *Boothbay Register*, 15 February 1908.

4. Francis Byran Greene, *History of Boothbay, Southport and Boothbay Harbor* (Somersworth, New Hampshire: New England History Press, 1984).

5. Ibid., 27.

6. Ibid.

7. Green, *Boothbay*, 336.

8. "Boothbay," *Boothbay Register*, 18 April 1908.

9. *Boothbay Register*, 9 May 1908.

10. Barbara Rumsey, executive secretary of the Boothbay Historical Society, letter to George King III, 5 January, 1994.

11. *Boothbay Register*, 9 May 1908.

12. John Ives Sewell, *Pictorial Supplement* (Christmas Cove, Maine: Christmas Cove Improvement Association, Spring 1966), printed as a supplement to *CCIA Notes*, 3.

13. *Murray & Tregurtha Company* (Boston: circa 1906), trade catalog.

14. U.S. Department of Commerce, *Annual Report of the Supervising Inspector-General, Steamboat Inspection Service*, fiscal year ending 30 June 1909, 139.

15. *Tregurtha*, 40.

16. *Merchant Vessel List*, 1920.

17. *Marine Engineering*, 1903.

18. *New London Day*, 19 June 1908.

19. *New London Day*, 10 February 1908, 3.

20. *New London Day*, 25 February 1908.

21. *New London Day*, 2 May 1908, 8.

22. N. Hawkins, comp., *Audels Mechanical Dictionary* (New York: Theo. Audel & Co., 1942), 370.

23. N. Hawkins, *Handbook of Calculations for Engineers and Firemen* (New York: Theo. Audel & Co., 1903), 161.

24. Ibid.

25. U.S. Customs, *Application to Collector of Customs for Official Number*, 14 May 1908.

26. *Laws of the United States Relating to the Measurement of Vessels*, Part 2. Measurement, (R.S. 4150-46 U.S.C. 74).

27. Customs, *Application*.

28. Harold W. Castner, "Damariscotta Steamboat Company," *Lincoln County News*, 11 September 1947.

29. *Boothbay Register*, 16 May 1908.

30. Commerce, *Annual Report*, 1909.

31. *Boothbay Register*, 6 June 1908.

32. David Crockett, "A Short History of the Steamer Sabino," *Steamboat Bill*, Spring 1968, 48-50.

33. *Lincoln County News*, 4 June 1908, 8.

34. *Boothbay Register*, advertisement; various dates through September 1908.

35. *Boothbay Register*, 6 July 1908, 3.

36. Timetable, Steamer *Tourist, Pemaquid Division*, 1 July 1912.

37. Ibid.

38. *C.C.I.A. Notes*.

39. Ibid.

40. Ibid.

41. Ibid.

42. Plan Showing the Route of the Damariscotta Stb't Co's daily line of Steamers, 1 June 1910.

43. *C.C.I.A. Notes*.

44. Telephone interview by author with RADM. William F. Royall USN (Ret.) 31 November 1994.

45. *Bath Daily Times*, 28 October 1921.

46. *Boothbay Register*, 14 June 1913.

47. *Boothbay Register*, 16 August 1913.

48. David Dodge et. al., *Steamboat Sabino* (Mystic, Connecticut: Mystic Seaport, Inc., 1974), 4.

49. *Boothbay Register*, 10 January 1914.

50. *Boothbay Register*, 28 March 1914.

51. U.S. Customs, *Admeasurement Document*, 1908.

52. Harold Castner, "Damariscotta Steamboat Company," *Lincoln County News*, 11 September 1947.

53. *Portland Press Herald*, as quoted in Harrison Brown, "Sabino Being Sold Down The Coast," *Evening Express*, (Portland, Maine: 5 April 1961).

54. *Boothbay Register*, 26 February 1915.

55. *Boothbay Register*, 22 October 1915.

56. *A Chronicle of the Automotive Industry in America 1893-1949* (Detroit: Automobile Manufacturers Association, 1949), 7 and 19.

57. Floyd Clymer, *Henry's Wonderful Model T* (New York: Bonanza Books, 1955), 134.

58. Floyd Clymer, *Treasury of Early American Automobiles 1877-1925* (New York: Bonanza Books, 1955), 179.

59. *Boothbay Register*, 16 June 1916.

60. Castner, "Steamboat."

61. *Maine State Register*, 1918-1919, 695.

62. *Boothbay Register*, 7 June 1918.

63. *Boothbay Register*, 14 June 1918.

CHAPTER FOUR

1. U.S. Department of Commerce and Labor, *Laws Governing the Steamboat-Inspection Service* (Washington, D.C.: U.S. Government Printing Office, 1908), 1.

2. U.S. Department of Commerce and Labor, *Laws Governing the Steamboat-Inspection Service* (Washington, D.C.: U.S. Government Printing Office, 1910), 59-61.

3. Ibid.

4. Commerce, *Laws*, 1908, 20, sec. 4438.

5. U.S. Department of Commerce, *Steamboat-Inspection Service Bulletin* (Washington, D.C.: 1 March 1916), vol. 5:1.

6. U.S. Department of Commerce, *Laws Governing the Steamboat-Inspection Service*, Title LII - Regulation of Steam Vessels, Section 441 - License of Engineer, Edition of 14 July 1917.

7. Ibid.

8. *Boothbay Register*, 19 May 1916.

9. *Record of Birth*, Everett Spear; Maine State Archives, Augusta, Maine.

10. *Vital Record*, Old Bristol and Nobleboro, Maine, vol. I, Births and Deaths, 645.

11. *Boothbay Register*, 31 March 1916.

12. Jim Millinger, "The Steamer Sabino on Casco Bay 1927-1961," *The Log of Mystic Seaport*, Autumn 1995, 61.

13. Harold W. Castner, "The Damariscotta Steamboat Company," *Lincoln County News*, 11 September 1947.

14. High tide was at 3:27 pm, which means that five to six knots of current was moving upstream with the boat.

15. Ibid.

16. Castner, "*Steamboat.*"

17. "Steamer Tourist Wrecked," unidentified newspaper (perhaps *Lincoln County News*), referring to the time of the accident as "Monday afternoon."

18. *C.C.I.A. Notes*.

19. "Wrecked."

20. Ibid.

21. Castner.

22. *C.C.I.A. Notes*.

23. Wreck Report, Str. *Tourist*, dated 21 November 1918.

24. "Wrecked."

25. *C.C.I.A. Notes*.

26. "Wrecked."

27. Record memorandum from Maynard Bray dated 13 March 1974 (Mystic Seaport registrar's file number L-73.187).

28. Letter from Jack Murry of East Boothbay, Maine, dated 4 October 1990.

29.. "Wrecked."

30. Interview with Spencer Gay by Mary Leonard 27 January 1974, from notes taken at the time and filed in registrar's office at Mystic Seaport (registrar's file number 73.187).

31. Bray.

32. "Wrecked."

33. *C.C.I.A. Notes*.

34. *Sheepscot Echo*, 30 August 1918.

35. "Wrecked."

36. Castner.

37. "Wrecked."

38. *Sheepscot Echo*, 30 August 1918.

39. "Wrecked."

40. *Boothbay Register*.

41. Record of Death, Everett Spear: Maine State Archives, Augusta, Maine.

42. *Boothbay Register*, 13 September 1918.

43. *Sheepscot Echo*, 20 September 1918, 1.

44. Manville W. Davis, New Harbor, Maine, letter to Mary Leonard dated 14 April 1974.

45. Wreck Report, Str. *Tourist*, 21 November 1918.

46. *Boothbay Register*, 15 November 1918.

47. *Boothbay Register*, 4 October 1918.

48. John Davenport, letter to Publications Department, Mystic Seaport, dated 24 October 1977.

49. Constance Rowe Lane, *Kennebec, Boothbay Harbor Steamboat Album* (Camden, Maine: Down East Enterprise, Inc., 1971), 35.

50. Captain William Frappier, *Steamboat Yesterdays on Casco Bay* (Toronto: Stoddart Publishing Company, Ltd., 1993), 144.

51. *Boothbay Register*, 14 March 1919, 5.

52. *Boothbay Register*, 13 June 1919.

53. Ibid.

54. *Boothbay Register*, 27 June 1919.

55. *Boothbay Register*, 25 July 1919.

56. *Boothbay Register*, 8 August 1919.

57. *Boothbay Register*, 13 June 1919, 5.

58. *Boothbay Register*, 15 August 1919.

59. *Boothbay Register*, 22 august 1919.

60. *Boothbay Register*, 11 June 1920.

61. *Boothbay Register*, 18 June 1920.

62. *Lincoln County News*, 24 June 1920.

63. *Johnson's Steam Vessels*, (New York: Eads John, M.E., Inc. 1921).

64. *Maine Register*, (Portland, Maine: Grenville M. Donham, 1919), 695.

65. *Maine Register*, 700.

66. *Lincoln County News*, 19 May 1921.

67. *Lincoln County News*, 5 May 1921.

68. *Maine Register*, 785.

69. *Lincoln County News*, 7 July 1921, 4.

70. *Lincoln County News*, 15 September 1921.

71. General Index or Abstract of Title, for steamer *Sabino*.

CHAPTER FIVE

1. William Avery Baker, *A Maritime History of Bath, Maine, and the Kennebec River Region* (Bath, Maine: Marine Research Society of Bath, 1973), 276.

2. Ibid.

3. W. Bartlett Cram, *Picture History of New England Passenger Vessels* (Hampden Highlands, Maine: Burncoat Corporation, 1980), 78.

4. Constance Rowe Land, *Kennebec, Boothbay Harbor Steamboat Album* (Camden, Maine: Down East Enterprise, Inc. 1971), 7.

5. Jane Stevens, *One Man's World, Popham Beach, Maine* (Freeport, Maine: Bond Wheelwright Co. 1974), 1.

6. *Popham Beach Steamboat Company*, (timetable), circa 1909.

7. Baker, *Kennebec*, 724.

8. Ibid.

9. Ibid., 726.

10. *Bath Sentinel*, 18 April 1889.

11. *Bath Independent*, 15 May 1886.

12. Baker, *Kennebec*, 734.

13. Ibid., 724.

14. Ibid.

15. *Bath Daily Times*, 15 April 1898.

16. Baker, *Kennebec*, 734.

17. Ibid., 724.

18. Ibid., 734.

19. Ibid., 727.

20. Byron M. Boyles, "Popham Beach Steamboat Company," *Steamboat Bill*, March 1950, 14-15.

21. Baker, *Kennebec*, 738.

22. General Index or Abstract of Title for steamer *Sabino*.

23. "Statement of Sale of Steamers," Popham Beach Steamboat Company records, 1921.

24. Stevens, *Popham*, 1.

25. Fannie Hardy Eckstorm, *Indian Places–Names of the Penobscot Valley and The Maine Coast* (Orono, Maine: University of Maine at Orono Press, 1978), 130.

26. Sir Ferdinando Gorges, *Relation of a Voyage to Sagadahoc 1607-1608* as quoted in *Gorges and the Grant of the Province of Maine, 1622* (State of Maine, 1923: 94).

27. Frederick Webb Hodge, ed., *Handbook of American Indians–North of Mexico* (1975), 400.

28. "Sale of Steamers," PBS Co.

29. *Bath Daily Times*, 28 October 1921.

30. *A Chronicle of the Automotive Industry in America 1893-1949* (Detroit: Automobile Manufacturers Association, 1949), 32.

31. Stevens, *Popham*, 91.

32. General Index or Abstract of Title for steamer *Sabino*.

CHAPTER SIX

1. *Casco Bay and Harpswell Lines*, timetable (Portland, Maine: Casco Bay and Harpswell Steamboat Co., 1911).

2. Peter T. McLaughlin, *The Casco Bay Islands* (Portland, Maine: Casco Bay Lines [undated] circa 1966).

3. *United States Coast Pilot I –Atlantic Coast –Eastport to Cape Cod.*

4. McLaughlin, *Islands*.

5. Jim Millinger, "The Steamer Sabino on Casco Bay 1927-1961," *The Log of Mystic Seaport*, Autumn 1995, 36.

6. Ibid.

7. Francis T. Bowles, ed. *Transactions of the Society of Naval Architects and Marine Engineers* (New York: Gibson Bros., 1898), plate 1-2.

8. Bill Durham, ed. *Steamboats and Modern Steam Launches* (Berkeley, California: Howell-North Books, March-April 1961), 20.

9. Millinger, *Sabino*, 36.

10. William J. Frappier, *Steamboat Yesterdays on Casco Bay* (Toronto: Stoddart Publishing Co. Ltd., 1993), 152-55.

11. Ibid.

12. General Index or Abstract of Title, for steamer *Sabino*.

13. Millinger, *Sabino*, 36.

14. *Portland Press Herald*, as quoted in Harrison Brown, "Sabino Being Sold Down The Coast," *Evening Express* (Portland, Maine: 5 April 1961).

15. John Ives Sewell, *Pictorial Supplement* (Christmas Cove, Maine: Association, Spring 1967 (printed as a supplement to *C.C.I.A. Notes*).

16. Millinger, *Sabino*, 36.

17. Ibid.

18. General Index or Abstract of Title, for steamer *Sabino*.

19. Millinger, *Sabino*, 36.

20. Frappier, *Yesterdays*, 75.

21. Ibid., 106.

22. Materials at Mystic Seaport, *Casco Bay Directory, 1933-35* and *Portland Directory, 1933-46*.

23. A photograph of *Sabino* taken on 30 August 1936 shows her before this change, *Portland Press Herald*, 31 August 1936.

24. This continued the evening service to Peaks initiated by Walter W. Kennedy's Island Night Service in 1921 and possibly offered by Harry William's Island Evening Line in the late 1920s; but *Sabino* was used only in the summertime.

25. Marie Zukunft Graves, interview with author (Millinger), summer 1993.

26. *Portland Evening Express*, 1 June 1946, and Robert and Agnes Hale, *Cushings Island*, 52.

27. These changes first show up pictorially in a photograph of *Sabino* in her wartime gray.

28. One informant remembers working the first "night" trip at 3:05 p.m., which was followed by runs at 5:10, 6:00, and 8:10 p.m. during the winter of 1942-43. Another informant, who was hookman of *Sabino* in the summers of 1944 and 1945, does not remember *Sabino* working in the winter months. However, he recalled that during the war Cliff Randall was employed in the winter by the Casco Bay Lines for the first time. This might well have been the winter when *Sabino* was used year-round.

29. Marie Zukunft Graves drew the distinction to my attention. She commented that she and her sisters were pursers, not mates. As an example of this, she told me that on the rare occasion when *Gurnet* (which carried a mate) replaced *Sabino*, Cliff Randall, as captain, came out of the pilothouse to heave the eye-spliced line. He never let her heave it. Did he consider it "unladylike," or did he think her not strong enough to heave it? Marie Zukunft Graves, interview with author (Millinger), summer 1993.

30. Clippings on file in the Portland Room of the Portland Public Library.

31. There was a major financial incentive to run *Sunshine* rather than *Sabino*. She only required a crew of two, rather than the four required on *Sabino*, and one licensed operator rather than two. The fuel costs undoubtedly were less.

32. *Portland Evening Express*, 4 September 1957.

33. Bruce Bruheld, interview with author (Millinger) summer 1993; *Portland Press Herald*, 4 September 1957.

34. *Portland Evening Express*, 19 September 1957.

35. One skipper informant told me (Millinger) that he was scheduled to take a charter trip on *Emita II*. When she was unable to go because of mechanical difficulties he took *Sabino*. Some tour-goers were outspoken in their disgust with the "smelly, dirty boat," despite his efforts to convince them that a ride aboard a steamer was a treat. Dunn, *Casco Bay Steamboat Album*, 28.

36. Eunice Randall Curran, interview with author (Millinger) summer 1993. Cliff Randall's obituary, *Portland Press Herald*, 5 October 1971, states that he retired in 1962. The *Portland Directory* listed him as "Captain 24 Custom House Wharf" through the 1960 edition. Article on his retirement, *Portland Press Herald*, 25 June 1963, states that he "retired about three years ago."

CHAPTER SEVEN

1. Note to Mystic Seaport from Peter McLaughlin, President of Casco Bay Lines, 25 August 1973.

2. General Index or Abstract of Title, steamer *Sabino*, New London, Connecticut, 14 November 1978.

3. *Portland Evening Express*, 5 April 1961.

4 Richard M. Mitchell, *The Steam Launch* (Camden, Maine: International Marine Publishing Co., 1982), 53.

5. Interview with John S. Clement, 16 November 1997.

6. W. Bartlett Cram, *Picture History of New England Passenger Vessels* (Hampden Highlands, Maine: Burncoat Corp., 1980), 202.

7. Doris Green, "Atlantic Seaboard." *Steamboat Bill*, Fall 1967, 139.

8. "The Intimate Steamboat," *Steamboat Bill*, Winter 1967, 214.

9. *Bordentown News*, 14 July 1971.

10. Telephone interview with Bruce Brown, 12 December 1997.

CHAPTER EIGHT

1. Recollections of Don Robinson, retired watercraft curator, Mystic Seaport, in telephone interview with author, December 1997

2. Maynard Bray, "Sabino Memories," e-mail to George King III dated 12 January 1998.

3. Interview with Mystic Seaport director, Revell Carr, 15 January 1998.

4. Ibid.

5. Bray.

6. Ibid.

7. Bareboat Charter between Steamship Sabino, Inc. and The Marine Historical Association, Inc. for period 1 January 1973 through 31 April 1974.

8. *Amesbury News*, 5 August 1971.

9. Bray.

10. Telephone interview with Bruce Brown, 12 December 1997.

11. Bray.

12. "Sabino Arrives," *The New London Day*, 9 May 1973

13. Robinson.

14. Robert W. Morse, "The Restoration/Reconstruction of the Steamboat *Sabino* at the DuPont Preservation Shipyard, Mystic Seaport 1974-1980."

15. David Dodge, "Report on the *Sabino*," 9 December 1974.

16. Ibid.

17. Ibid.

CHAPTER NINE

1. *Sabino* log 1974; Collection 232, Box 7, G.W. Blunt White Library, Mystic Seaport.

2. Ibid.

3. Don Cawley, "*Sabino* Captain." *The New London Day*, 1976.

4. *Sabino*, log, 1974.

5. *Dresser News*, Stratford, Connecticut, 1974.

6. *Sabino* log, 1977. Collection 232, Box 7, G.W. Blunt White Library, Mystic Seaport.

7. Ibid.

8. Peter T. Vermilya, "Restoration/Reconstruction of the Pilot House."

PLANS

(LARGER-SCALE VERSIONS OF THESE DRAWINGS MAY BE ORDERED FROM
SHIPS PLANS, MYSTIC SEAPORT, P.O. BOX 6000, MYSTIC, CT 06355-0990)

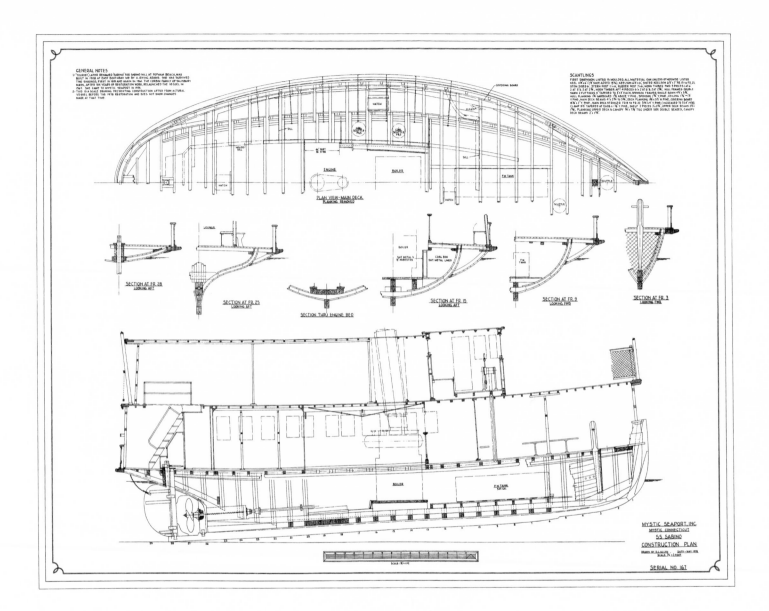

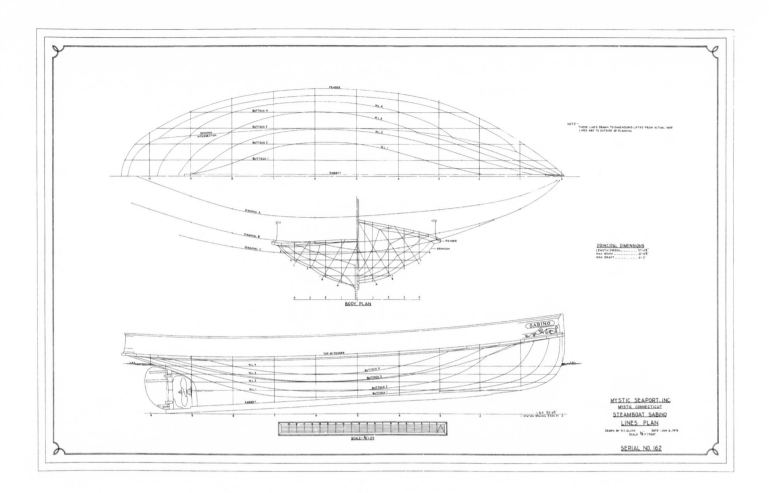

PRINCIPAL DIMENSIONS
LENGTH OVERALL _____ 57-08"
MAX BEAM _____ 21-08"
MAX DRAFT _____ 6-3"

BODY PLAN

MYSTIC SEAPORT, INC.
MYSTIC CONNECTICUT
STEAMBOAT SABINO
LINES PLAN
DRAWN BY R.C.ALLYN   DATE: JAN 6, 1976
SCALE 3/8 = 1 FOOT

SERIAL NO. 162

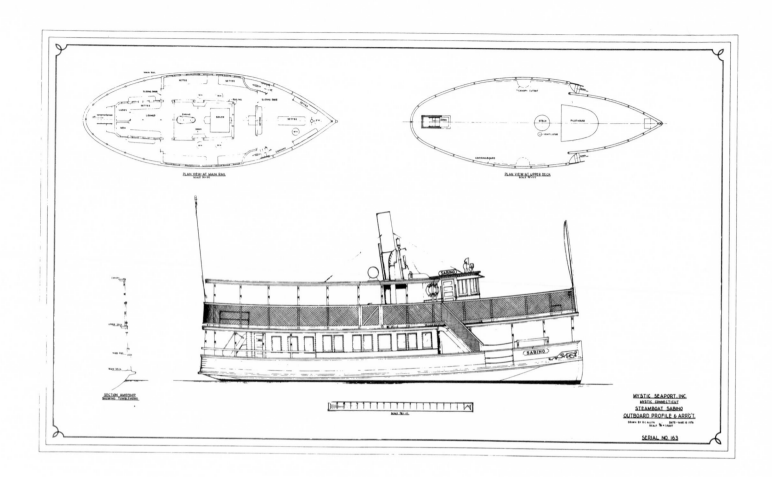

PLAN VIEW-AT MAIN RAIL
SCALE 3/4" = 1'

PLAN VIEW-AT UPPER DECK
SCALE 3/4" = 1'

SECTION AMIDSHIP
SHOWING TUMBLEHOME

SCALE 3/4" = 1'

MYSTIC SEAPORT, INC.
MYSTIC CONNECTICUT
STEAMBOAT SABINO
OUTBOARD PROFILE & ARR'G'T.
DRAWN BY D.C.ALLYN   DATE - MAR. 10 1976
SCALE 3/4" = 1 FOOT

SERIAL NO. 163

124 PLANS

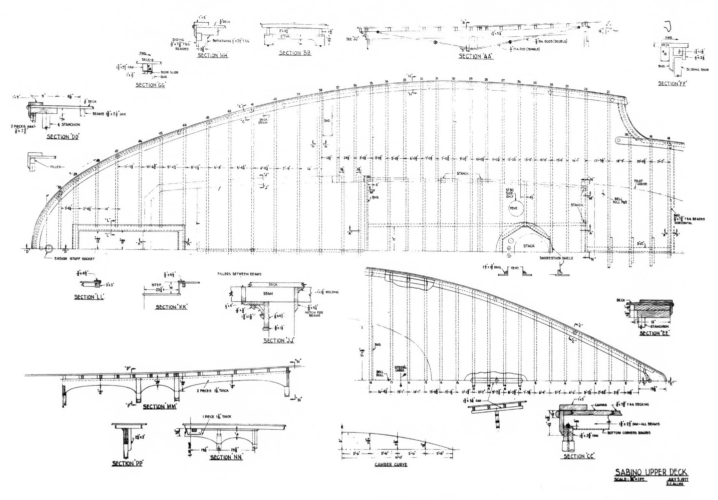

SECTION "HH"

SECTION "BB"

SECTION "AA"

SECTION "FF"

SECTION "GG"

SECTION "DD"

SECTION "EE"

SECTION "LL"

SECTION "KK"

SECTION "JJ"

SECTION "MM"

SECTION "PP"

SECTION "NN"

CAMBER CURVE

SECTION "CC"

SABINO UPPER DECK
SCALE: ¾"=1FT.   JULY 5, 1977
R.C. ALLYN

SK. No. 199

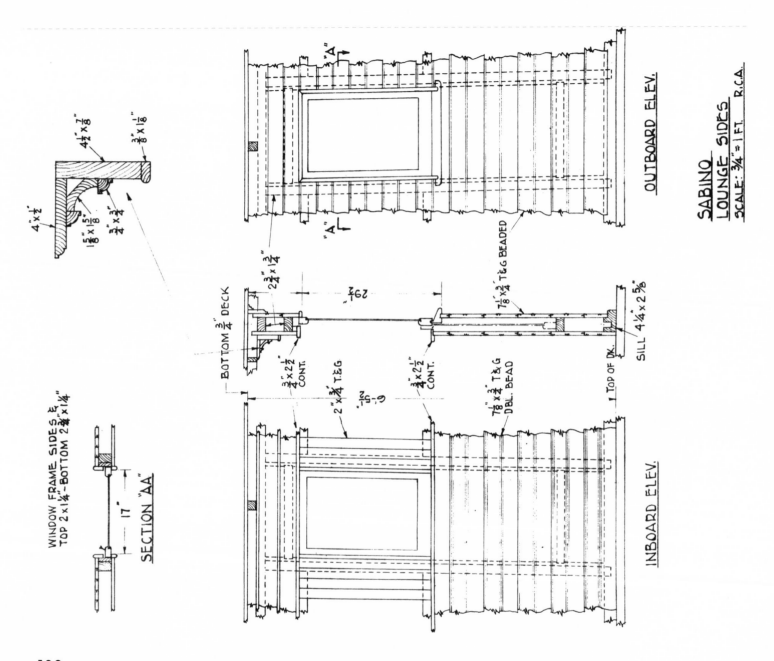

OUTBOARD ELEV.

SABINO
LOUNGE SIDES
SCALE: ¾" = 1 FT.   R.C.A.

INBOARD ELEV.

$4\frac{1}{2}"\times\frac{7}{8}"$

$\frac{3}{8}"\times 1\frac{1}{8}"$

$4"\times\frac{1}{2}"$

$1\frac{5}{8}"\times 1\frac{5}{8}"$

$\frac{3}{4}"\times\frac{3}{4}"$

WINDOW FRAME SIDES & ⅛
TOP 2"×1¼"-BOTTOM 2¾"×1¼"

SECTION "AA"

17"

$2\frac{3}{4}"\times 1\frac{3}{4}"$

29¼"

BOTTOM ¾ DECK

$\frac{3}{4}"\times 2\frac{1}{2}"$ CONT.

2"×¾" T&G

$\frac{3}{4}"\times 2\frac{1}{2}"$ CONT.

$7\frac{1}{8}"\times\frac{3}{4}"$ T&G BEADED

SILL 4¼ × 2⅝

$7\frac{1}{8}"\times\frac{3}{4}"$ T&G
DBL. BEAD

6'-5½"

TOP OF DK.

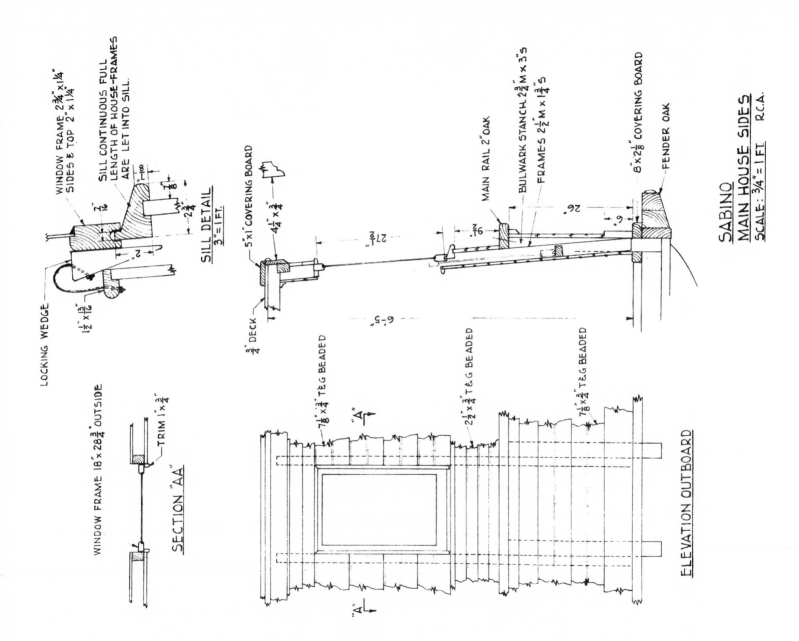

WINDOW FRAME $2\frac{3}{4}$" x $1\frac{1}{4}$"
SIDES & TOP 2" x $1\frac{1}{4}$"

SILL CONTINUOUS FULL
LENGTH OF HOUSE-FRAMES
ARE LET INTO SILL.

$\frac{7}{16}$"

$\frac{1}{8}$"

$2\frac{1}{4}$"

$\frac{7}{16}$"

LOCKING WEDGE

2"

$1\frac{1}{2}$" x $1\frac{3}{16}$"

SILL DETAIL
$\frac{3}{4}$" = 1 FT.

5 x 1" COVERING BOARD

$4\frac{1}{4}$" x $\frac{3}{4}$"

$\frac{3}{4}$" DECK

$27\frac{1}{2}$"

MAIN RAIL 2" OAK

$\frac{7}{16}$"

BULWARK STANCH. $2\frac{3}{4}$" M x 3"S

FRAMES $2\frac{1}{2}$" M x $1\frac{3}{4}$"S

26"

6"

8" x $2\frac{1}{8}$" COVERING BOARD

FENDER OAK

6'-5"

WINDOW FRAME 18" x $28\frac{3}{4}$" OUTSIDE

TRIM 1" x $\frac{3}{4}$"

SECTION "AA"

$7\frac{1}{8}$" x $\frac{3}{4}$" T&G BEADED

$2\frac{1}{2}$" x $\frac{3}{4}$" T&G BEADED

$7\frac{1}{8}$" x $\frac{3}{4}$" T&G BEADED

"A"

"A"

ELEVATION OUTBOARD

SABINO
MAIN HOUSE SIDES
SCALE: $\frac{3}{4}$" = 1 FT   R.C.A.

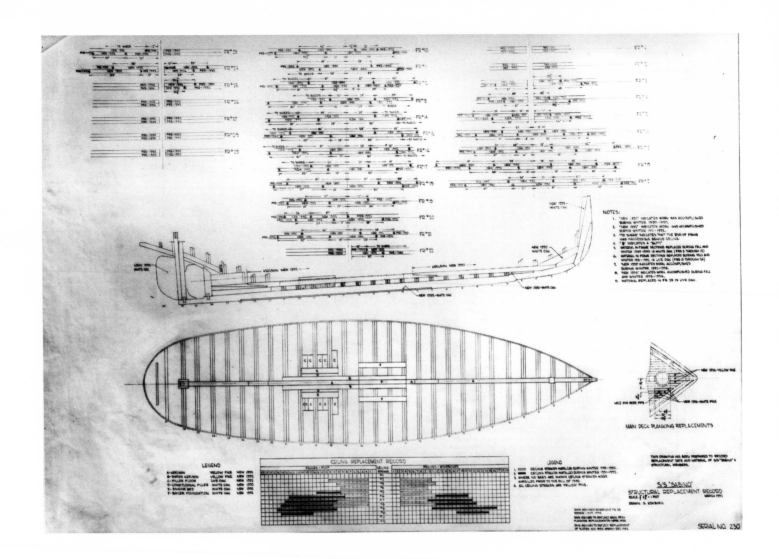

MAIN DECK PLANKING REPLACEMENTS

S/S "SABINO"
STRUCTURAL REPLACEMENT RECORD

SERIAL NO. 230

INDEX

Page numbers in *italics* indicate illustrations. Numbers followed by 'n' indicate notes.